WINX

The Problem-Solving Model to Win Exponentially with Customers, Employees, & Your Bottom Line

Irma Parone

ISBN: 979-8-9861969-0-9

Contents

How to Use This Book

You might be wondering if this book is a problem-solving model or a method to WIN EXPONENTIALLY with Customers, Employees, and Your Bottom Line. The answer is—Yes! (Both).

None of us wake up one day, wave a wand, and know everything we need to 'fix things.' Instead, life successes and failures are typically a mix of journeys. These journeys form our opinions, strategies, and even our personality traits.

Combining and connecting my experiences with a tremendous amount of research, plus, a little help from my friends, I present to you a model that will create a shift in how you see problems, assess the impact of those problems, and then identify solutions that result in wins in your personal and business life.

My best recommendations for using this book are to first read through each chapter and download the WINX forms for easy access. Then get started! The download links are provided later in this book.

Common Questions

Q: Why read the entire book before working on a project?

A: As you read through the book, you will absorb an array of ideas that correspond to various steps, and a deeper understanding of Winning Exponentially.

Q: What if my business does not include customers, but rather students or patients?

A: No problem! In the WINX download for problem-solving, you can easily edit the titles. For example, instead of customers, employees, and company, you might override them with student, faculty, and organization, or patients, staff and organization, and so on. Easily convert to your industry!

Q: Remote working has become the norm for some companies; how would you apply this model in remote decision-making and problem-solving?

A: Collaboration should be relatively easy as many remote meeting platforms include audio, video, whiteboard, screen sharing, and the ability to organize documents. In addition, our WINX download form is reusable and allows you to identify company names with plenty of room to add each specific location, such as Parone Group - Ft Lauderdale. Each location's submission will be clearly identified for easy review.

Q: Do I need to follow all eight steps and in order?

A: No. Once you understand the process and reason for each step, you can choose what works for you, your industry, or the particular problem. There is, however, one step that I recommend considering for every problem and idea you are working through. Making a habit of Step 5 at every level of your organization will shift your culture, one problem, idea, or suggestion at a time.

Saying that, some challenges (problems) will go away on their own, and some don't need a lengthy process. Other decisions will be emotional, personal, easy, fast, "no-brainer" decisions. Still, other decisions will take weeks, months, or years to research and implement. These will require returning to each step multiple times.

Q: There are a lot of ideas for problem-solving in this book. How do I choose?

A: Review them all and choose what works best for you. You may use your top three, or you might find using different ideas for varying problems works.

Of course, you could also write each tool on separate pieces of paper, put them in a jar, shake it, open the lid, and throw them up in the air. Use which lands first! (*Just kidding!*).

WINX is about giving you options, not forcing you to "play by the rules." However, as the famous tradesman's mantra says, I urge you to, "Learn the trade before learning the 'tricks of the trade' if you want to make successful decisions." Then go for it. You will make it your own!

For a free WINX self-assessment tool that may be fun and informational before you start this book, go to www.ParoneGroup. com/WINXAssessment. We will also provide updates on future publications, as these publications will be written specifically for your employees, customers, vendors, or others.

You are ready to go. Each problem is different, and with practice, the better you will become at taking the steps that make the most sense to you, naturally.

I hope you enjoy the book, learn a lot, and share your lessons learned. Thank you, and happy reading! Let's go!

Introduction

Why do we have jobs? Your business plans or job descriptions include words such as create, manage, plan, develop, and so on. I suspect, however, you created your business or were hired in large part to solve or prevent problems. It is therefore important to understand, like it or not, many decisions are *emotional*—driven by a combination of inputs from what the late physician and neuroscientist Paul McLean called our "Triune Brain: the 1) basal ganglia, 2) the limbic system, and 3) the neocortex."

Scientists differ over the correct evolution of the brain's systems, but the Triune Brain model still offers the most straightforward and best examples of how humans *process* their lives. Recent technological advances in brain imaging show activity in several brain regions during primal, emotional, and rational experiences. Each of these is perceived as responsible for specific mental activities, including 1) The fight-or-flight survival response as well as other primal activities, 2) emotions, and 3) rational thinking.

In this book, I share the insights I have gained from my research on making better decisions. I also bring in my extensive corporate

Introduction

background, ongoing developmental education, and consulting experience to combine the process of decision-making with a culture of winning in the workplace. You can Google "How to make a decision" and find hundreds, if not thousands, of articles, lists, and how-to videos on the subject. But many will not mention the critical limbic (emotional) aspect of the decision-making process, even though our emotions, conscious or not, contribute significantly to every decision we make.

In fact, the decision-making part of our brains is so connected to the limbic (emotion generating) part of our brain that if that system is damaged somehow (disease, accident, drugs, etc.), it will literally render us unable to make any decision.[1] Research has consistently shown that even in the smallest of decisions, our emotions are involved.[2]

Alan Sanfey, a cognitive neuroscientist at the University of Arizona, and his colleagues used fMRI scans to look into people's brains while these participants played "the ultimatum game," a game where participants are pitted against each other in a simple negotiation.

Player One has $10 and is tasked with splitting the money with a second player—the recipient. Let's say you are the recipient. Player one can offer you any amount, from zero to $10, and Player One gets to keep the change—but only if you accept the offer. Any offer may be rejected, but if you choose to do so, neither player gets anything. Both players know, before playing the game, the consequences of the recipient accepting or rejecting the offer.

No matter how much or little is offered, you should accept the offer. After all, getting some money is better than getting none. Simple, right? Not exactly. In an article by the *Harvard Business Review*, Gardiner Morse wrote that when the offer dwindles to a few dollars, people on the receiving end consistently turn it down. He explained that they are willing to forfeit "… a free couple of bucks for—well, for what, exactly? Recipients will ultimately tell researchers they rejected the lowball offer because they were ticked off at the stingy or greedy partner (who, remember, loses her share, too). Not exactly a triumph of reason. This sounds like the dog brain at work, and it is." [3]

This same process, conscious or unconscious, is at work across every decision we make. Whether it's personal or professional—our emotional issues or mindset work hand-in-hand to complement, shore up, or derail all of our decisions. Even just being aware that this emotional influence is going on can improve your decision-making process. The bottom line here? The more you understand how you make decisions and how to make decisions, the better you can manage the outcome. [4]

Good, Bad, Ugly, or Awesome; We Are the Decisions We Make

"I am not a product of my circumstances. I am a product of my decisions."

— Stephen Covey

We make thousands of decisions every day. From the start of your day, where you decide whether to have that health shake (good) or donut (not so good) to whether you will stay at home or drive to work —you're making decisions.

Larger decisions—like how to spend your time or money, or whether to fire that problem employee or bring in a coach to help him/her improve, whether to move forward or sign a contract now or later, occupy our time as well. Large or small, significant or not, we make decisions every day, usually without thinking much about the process. After all, we've been making decisions all our lives and we're pretty good at it—or so most of us believe.

But how often do we think about how we can make *better decisions?* *Better decisions* are decisions that, well made, help us move through a more thoughtful *process* that results in our producing the best outcomes possible for us, our employees, customers, and our business. Focused decision-making makes for better business, whether you're a solopreneur, a small business, or in the C-suite of a corporation.

I have found that business leaders make better decisions by focusing on the impact of their decisions on what I call "The Focused Trio." In my world, the service industry, this trio is composed of your customers, your employees, and your company. However, many of us only think about the impact on just one of our stakeholders—your company, or two—your company and your customers. But something even more productive happens when you consider all of your stakeholders. In this book, I'll show you the methodology I use and how it can help you make better decisions.

THE FOCUSED TRIO

From a labor relations manager in a union intense environment to a general manager, to a senior vice president and later, a consultant, I have had the honor of helping companies and their leaders take better care of customers, employees, and company by learning to master making more thoughtful, strategic decisions. I laid out this program into a concise and easy-to-follow eight-step process I use and call "Winning Exponentially" or simply: "WINX."

I'm confident that once you go through the eight steps I share in this book, you'll begin to understand the logic and practicality of this approach. These steps, along with a wide variety of real-life stories and examples that illustrate how to master the eight steps of WINX, will better equip you to rally with deeper insight, awareness, and optimism when presented with problems.

Positive, yet strategic wins will help you develop more productive, engaged, and successful employees. It's far easier to direct and inspire the minds of those around you to collaborate when they are optimistic and involved.

If you Google "decision making," you'll see the process itself is pretty simple. It's not rocket science. So why do so many of us continue to make bad decisions? Because there is no such thing as a purely rational self.

Research has proven time and time again that decision-making is intrinsically linked to our emotions. We are emotional creatures who deny and even flaunt or ignore reason and rationality.

The stories I share throughout this book will reflect this fact. Even CEO thought-leaders, and others with brilliant minds, will make decisions based on *emotional reactions* such as spite, a desire to please, or anger.

Yet unless we're making decisions as objectively as possible, we're more likely than not to make bad decisions—even while knowing what the good decision was—as thousands of companies have done.

However, the good news is that becoming aware of your emotions as you make your decisions will enable you to more effectively control your choices and achieve better results.

How Small Bad Decisions Become Big, Bad Decisions

A friend of mine was working in a small local grocery store and noticed a puddle of water outside a freezer compartment. It was a small puddle, so employees simply mopped it up without evaluating the problem. They addressed the symptom of the problem, but they didn't look for the source of the leak. This went on for a week. One morning the puddle was gone, but the freezer had broken overnight. On closer examination, the water was coming from a cracked water line. Once the line was empty, the freezer broke.

Had the store taken the time to find the source of the leak, the store could have avoided having to throw away a freezer full of half-thawed food, as well as the much higher cost of repairs. What looked like a small problem was the symptom of a much larger one. *Not all problems can be adequately addressed in terms of impact at first glance.* That's why assessing the impact of what appears to simply be a small problem can be critical in heading off much larger problems. This one seemingly small problem could have easily put this small grocery store out of business. Why, with such a seemingly small problem? Because this owner was already struggling and near bankruptcy.

> *"People say that it's the big decisions that are important... that these are the type of issues worthy of prolonged consideration. But no one ever explains how the little choices send your life careening in another direction."*
>
> *— Julie Gittus*

Blockbuster Video had over 9,000 video and DVD rental stores worldwide and annual revenue of close to $6 billion when Netflix—a relatively young company—offered them $50 million to help them launch their DVD-by-mail service.

Blockbuster laughingly decided to decline the offer. Who's laughing now? Blockbuster has disappeared from the market entirely while Netflix's market value is nearing $200 billion.[1] Why? They made a poorly researched, emotional response to their disappearing market share. They failed to take Netflix's offer seriously. Blockbuster assumed that streaming videos would never catch on like many famous failures. It didn't take long for the market to prove them wrong. But they still failed to act.

When Blockbuster realized that the paradigm for video rental was changing, they didn't take time to reconsider their assumptions, then gather facts to inform a sound action plan to reclaim their vanishing market share.

They responded in an emotional manner—copying rather than innovating. They tried to copy Netflix's red boxes and other models—to the extent that Netflix sued them for copyright infringement.[2]

"Rather than charting a course and remaining consistent, they bounced from one plan to another, following instead of leading the pack. Those ever-changing initiatives drained the company of precious resources that could have provided a reserve to help them ride out the storm," Encore Life Skills, LLC noted in their blog.[3]

I, along with many business leaders, believe a rational, well-researched decision-making model would have given executives evidence that supported Netflix's findings while also providing a chance to make a better decision, albeit one after the fact. It just might have kept them from going bankrupt and disappearing. We'll never know.

A thousand opinions, research models, and studies will explain why Blockbuster made the wrong decision. Still, I'm *curious how they framed their problem—or if they even examined the offer—for their decision to be so bad.* In reading various case studies about the decision and the resulting panic as Netflix took over their market, I have found that it was a very emotionally driven decision—as were the actions that followed.

What seemed to them like "just another business decision" would ultimately become the decision that led to their demise. It's not the size of the decision that matters as much as the ripples that decision generates.

How you and your company craft your "problem statement" and what emotions you pay attention to matter when making any size decision. For instance:

Back in 1982, Steven Spielberg offered the Mars Company the opportunity to feature their popular product, M&Ms in the movie *E.T.* The movie would become one of the most iconic films of all time, something nobody could have foreseen (or could they?), but Mars declined—saying they believed the alien, E.T., was "ugly and scary and would frighten the children who liked their product and result in a drop in sales."[4]

Hershey, however, jumped at the offer. They agreed on a $1 million product placement deal to push their Reese's Pieces product in the movie. The subsequent exposure of Reese's Pieces was worth an estimated $20 million to Hershey. Quite a windfall. Wow.[5]

I've often wondered, did Hershey see an *opportunity* in the movie *E.T.*, while the Mars Company only saw *a threat* to their existing customer base? Did it all boil down to an emotional aversion to the looks of the plastic character who was the beloved star of the movie, or was it something else? I believe emotions had a lot to do with the ultimate decision. Yoda was no male model, and most of the hobbits wouldn't turn heads with longing if they walked into a bar with those hairy feet and adorable round faces. Shrek was no beauty, yet the princess (and audiences) loved him. *Beauty and the Beast, Frankenstein... the list continues. As we've seen repeatedly, audiences love an ugly underdog, and most of that is tied to our emotions.*

And while the Mars/Hershey story is fascinating, there's more to Hershey's than most people realize. After making that one brilliant and timely decision, they failed to make another, more obvious (and also emotional) decision that led to a tremendous loss—just a reminder that even iconic companies make good and bad decisions. It's how life and business work. We learn more from our failures and bad decisions than from our good ones.

First of all, Milton Hershey, founder of the Hershey Chocolate Company, failed at two companies before starting his candy kingdom. He had experienced massive failures and learned from them—a good thing.

Most companies regularly make good and bad decisions, but often, the bad decisions are the ones they could've seen coming, and often did, but chose to ignore the obvious.

When Hershey decided to switch over its $112 million IT system, their worst-case scenarios became a reality.

According to PEMCO Consulting Services, who published a case study on the incident, "Hershey set out to upgrade its patchwork of IT systems into an integrated Enterprise Resource Planning environment in 1999." PEMCO pointed out in their analysis that the company chose the right software. However, in a rush (emotional) to "get it done," they ignored the experts' instructions on implementing it correctly. Despite a recommended implementation time of forty-eight months (four years), Hershey demanded a thirty-month (two-and-a-half years) turnaround to roll out the systems before the now-infamous Y2K and a much worried about computer glitch when computer counters hit the year 2000.

The result? Business process and systems issues created an operational paralysis, leading to a 19 percent drop in quarterly profits and an 8 percent decline in stock price"—all due to one very critical and poorly made decision where the company knew better but chose to ignore the experts it hired.

But wait. Ignoring the recommended rollout time to push something through wasn't a poor enough decision. Rather than wait for a slower time of the year to make the cut, the switch was planned for July 1999. This made their go-live scheduling coincide with Hershey's busiest periods—the time during which it would receive the bulk of its Halloween and Christmas orders.[6]

There's more. PEMCO pointed out that to meet the shorter deadline, Hershey's implementation team also had to cut corners on critical systems testing phases to meet the aggressive and not-recommended scheduling demands.

When the new systems went live in July 1999, unforeseen issues from the lack of testing prevented orders from flowing through the systems. As a result, Hershey could not process $100 million worth of Kiss and Jolly Rancher orders, even though the company had most of the inventory in stock.[7]

What impressed me about PEMCO's analysis is this statement:

"This is not one of those 'hindsight is 20/20' cases. In Hershey's position, a reasonably prudent implementer would never have permitted cutover under those circumstances."

PEMCO said, *"Not a genius, not a gifted expert,"* simply *"a reasonably prudent implementer."*

In other words, after analyzing and looking at the decisions that needed to be made, any rational, prudent person understanding the potential for serious issues would never have allowed the company to switch (cut) over under the circumstances.

Yet, someone did, and the result was "Hershey's implementation team made the cardinal mistake of sacrificing systems testing for the sake of expediency."[8] Remember this when you get to the last step of the WINX process—implementation.

Contrast that poor decision with the process where Hershey saw opportunity, not a threat, in positioning their Reese's Pieces in an unknown movie about a space alien.

I would have loved to have been in the room at both companies during their decision-making process! Those two options—threat vs. opportunity are polar opposites. Consider the questions to pose here, such as:

- Who made the decision at Hershey?
- Who turned down the chance at Mars?
- More importantly, what was the decision-making process like, and how much did the process rely on emotions rather than data, experience, or facts?
- What was the problem statement?
- Why did it change years later in relation to ignoring an IT implementation schedule?

I share these questions regarding these two decisions to show you that just because one person or company makes one inspired and brilliant decision at some point in time, it doesn't mean all the decisions are equally accurate or good. How could they be?

We are all human, all emotional, and all fallible, and every decision brings different challenges.

Decision-making is a science, a practice, but it is not an exact science and, as we know, it's very much connected to our emotions, to how we feel on a given day or time.

You're more likely to make the best decision if you can set aside strong emotions or incorporate them with the researched facts, and then select the wisest alternatives. If you ignore reality, ignore experts (in this case IT experts), and "sacrifice testing and science in the name of expediency," your track record will take some serious hits.

Hershey recovered despite the bad decision, but the business world is full of companies that didn't.

Many of these potential outcomes couldn't be seen at the time, but time has proven that many others could. Perhaps a combination of ego, emotions, arrogance, and the failure to accurately and adequately identify or explore the problem and alternatives resulted in the famous outcomes we now see with so many corporations and even individuals, as the following story will illustrate.

From J.K. Rowling to Bill Gates

J.K. Rowling, author, and creator of the *Harry Potter* series, was turned down by eleven publishers before the 12th publisher accepted her book—paying her a £1,500 advance ($2,000 US), or a total of roughly $4,100 in 1997 dollars. In 2021, the *Sunday Times* Rich List estimated Rowling's fortune at £820 million, ranking her as the 196th richest person in the UK. The rest is history, of course.

Over 500 million copies of her *Harry Potter* series have been sold, making it the bestselling book series of all time. *Harry Potter and the Sorcerer's Stone* (the first book of the series) sold more than 120 million copies. To date, the Harry Potter movies are the highest-grossing film series of all time. And, J.K. Rowling is the first author to earn more than $1 billion. In 2021 alone, she earned an estimated $54 million from books, movies, theme parks, and stage productions.[9]

But Rowling didn't have a smooth path of intelligent decisions to get to that point. Over several years, she actually made a string of bad decisions based on her emotions to get to the point where she started making good decisions.

Her "bad" decisions included setting the first Harry Potter book aside to pursue a relationship that ultimately ended badly. Deciding to move from the UK to Portugal on a whim was what many described as a rash, emotional decision. Perhaps her worst decision, one she says she regrets deeply, is not telling her mother about her Harry Potter books before her mother passed away.[10]

Yet, despite her poor and emotional decisions, her books went on to be incredibly successful. Why? Because she made better decisions *as she learned from her bad ones*. Not everyone gets that second chance, and those opportunities and people we reject with our decisions often benefit or succeed far more than we, or they, imagined. It's not that our emotions, or that making emotional decisions is wrong. Emotions can play a critical and positive role in our decision-making if we're aware of them.

Was it Bill Gates' youth (age 23) in 1979 that led American IT company Electronic Data Systems (EDS) to decide not to invest in Microsoft?[11] Gates had already proven his value and worth. In business only three years at the time of his offer to EDS, he'd already made a million dollars that year. He wasn't exactly living in his parent's basement and delivering pizza on the weekends.

At the time, EDS was worth around $1 billion and was looking to invest in a small computer company to supply them with valuable software. According to *CEO Today Magazine*, Microsoft was one of the options they considered, but EDS ultimately refused to meet Gates' asking price of $40–60m. I find it interesting that Gates refused to drop his price—often an emotional response to a potential client/customer walking away.

Microsoft is now worth more than one trillion dollars, and EDS no longer exists. The company became defunct in 2009, fifty years after it was founded.[12] Did EDS carefully examine the value Gates was offering, or decline because of an emotional response—what they perceived as "too much money" or Gates' age and brashness?[13] Microsoft was very successful at the time, and given the potential value of his product to EDS, his $40–60m asking price was not unreasonable. So why did EDS decide not to buy Microsoft?

What other decisions led to EDS's rise and fall over the years following their decision not to buy Microsoft? More importantly, how did Gates' decision not to accept less than what he considered his company's value become a smart decision—one not driven by fear of not making a sale?

The consequences of our decisions may be immediate or not appear for decades—especially in business transactions. But even small, personal decisions to start or stop drinking, smoking, getting fit, or dating have consequences that may not be obvious—at least until you develop cancer, lose weight, or meet your soulmate. You may discover you're glad you took that chance, that detour, that class, or attended that function you thought you'd loathe—but met your future spouse at.

"Life," as gamblers say, is a "crapshoot," a game of chances. That "obvious" choice you meant for good, is just as likely to destroy you as make you a success—or is it? So how can we make decisions that don't destroy us, our company, or those around us? We make them using the WINX decision-making model.

Following is an example of the unintended *negative* consequences that can also impact your personal connections—close and extended family, etc. when making quick and even rash decisions.

Lottery Winner? Think Twice

In 2019, a South Carolina woman decided to go on a scenic drive during her downtime on a business trip to Greenville. Her attorney later told the media she was "driving past a KC Mart when its 'signs about the jackpot caught her eye,' and she decided to stop in and 'buy a ticket.'"

Those two fairly benign, but emotional decisions—to "go for a drive, and to stop to buy a lottery ticket," would result in a remarkably unintended windfall. The woman, who chose to remain anonymous, became the largest Mega Millions jackpot lottery winner in the history of the lottery, collecting $1.5 billion for her spur-of-the-moment decision.

In December 2021, as I was writing this book, James Miller of Iron Station, NC, also made a "spur-of-the-moment decision" to buy Powerball tickets. His small investment became a life-changing moment when he won $100,000 in the Saturday drawing. He told Powerball officials, *"Six dollars changed my life.* I've got two babies at home, and they sure are going to have an amazing Christmas now."

As I researched these so-called "decisions," I noticed more and more that the majority of lottery winners across the country acted on a whim, a "feeling," or a gut instinct they couldn't explain, rather than on a structured decision-making process.[14]

These weren't huge, prolonged, or complex decisions. Most involved only a fleeting thought, a few seconds, and a few dollars or less. These spur-of-the-moment decisions were totally based on whims but still had tremendous impacts. If these people hadn't won, their decision not to play, for instance, wouldn't be worth mentioning. Either way, their decisions would still have consequences—just smaller ones.

When I spoke with friends about these spur-of-the-moment decisions that resulted in significant life changes, the reactions were mixed.

"I wish I could make a great spur-of-the-moment decision like that!" most said. But another friend, a more seasoned businesswoman, shrugged and said, "That's probably the only good decision they'll make about the lottery. Multi-millionaires or not, the money will be gone within five years, and they'll be broke, declare bankruptcy, or constantly bleed money."

At first, I didn't believe her, but I found out she was right. Winning a lot of money only postpones or guarantees bankruptcy for most winners. It doesn't prevent it. Lottery winners are much more likely to declare bankruptcy within three to five years after winning millions than the average American who hasn't won money or come into a financial windfall.

"Evidence shows that most people who make it to the top one percent of income earners usually don't stay at the top for very long," writes Jonnelle Marte, a reporter for *The Washington Post*.[15]

Economist Jay L. Zagorsky agrees. In an article for the US *News and World Report*, he wrote: "Studies found that instead of getting people out of financial trouble, winning the lottery got people into *more* trouble since bankruptcy rates soared for lottery winners three to five years after winning."

He also pointed out that research suggests many people who do win a lottery, or even inherit a lot of money or come into any financial windfall, quickly spend it—a result of many poor or outright bad decisions after collecting their win. A 2001 paper (by economists Guido Imbens and Bruce Sacerdote and statistician Donald Rubin) found that lottery winners saved just sixteen cents of every dollar they won.[16]

Other studies found that instead of getting people out of financial trouble, winning the lottery got people into more financial and personal trouble—why? *Because of the decisions, many of them emotional, they made after winning.*

Jack Whittaker won $315 million in a lottery in West Virginia in 2002, yet he now wishes he hadn't. He told *Time Magazine*, "I wish that we had torn the ticket up." After winning the money, life drastically changed for him and his family. His daughter and granddaughter both died due to drug overdoses related to the sudden wealth.[17]

I was fascinated to learn all this because it simply reinforced for me what I've believed all along—that our successes and failures in life *are directly related to the decisions we make: that good decisions can ultimately result in bad outcomes, and bad decisions can ultimately result in good outcomes, and that even making no decision is still a decision.*

My WINX process is, at its heart, all about decisions—the ones we make, the ones we don't make, the ones we wish we'd made, the ones we wish we could "make over."

I share this story here, early in this book, to help you gain a personal understanding of better decision-making, as most of us can understand buying a lottery ticket. Regardless of your race, age, gender, ethnicity, financial status, or background, most of us can identify with the random "decision" to buy a lottery ticket. Most of us won't see it as a serious decision at all—but as "following a hunch." And that's the hook. The things in our lives that can and often do change us for life begin as simple, careless, innocent, and often emotionally driven decisions. We are lulled into thinking and believing that we're smart enough, savvy enough, experienced enough, and competent enough to make any decision because we've been making decisions our entire lives.

Sure, we've all made some bad decisions, but who hasn't? You deal with it and move on. You do the best you can with what you know at the time and just hope, or pray, that you made the best choice out of the alternatives you had to choose from.

Besides, you tell yourself: consequences are consequences whether we spend a lot of time making the decision, or if we decide on a whim, or spin a wheel or roll the dice, or flip a coin. Does that mean making thoughtful, calculated decisions doesn't matter any more than careless, spur-of-the-moment decisions? No! While the lottery winners did make spontaneous decisions that resulted in a win, their decisions after the fact were actually poorly made. As a result, these decisions resulted in negative consequences.

Those winners who sought expert advice made wise decisions and invested well were usually able to keep their money and their new lifestyles. Those who continued to make decisions "by the seat of their pants," or trusting in their own wisdom or "insight" were the ones who suffered. My point is:

> *Every decision we make, every problem we solve, or issue we act on —changes us and/or those around us in some meaningful way. It may be a decision as simple as changing the time we get up, to the employees we hire, or fire, or when and how we fire them. But it's still a decision and should be undertaken with forethought and awareness. Decisions made with care, concern, examination, and a well-crafted problem statement result in the most consistent and best long-term decisions.*

I'm not saying you won't make bad decisions if you follow my formula. *I'm saying you won't make nearly as many bad decisions if you do.* You'll be better prepared for the fallout, more likely to recoup your losses and move on, and more likely to make a better decision the next time. Most importantly, by researching and examining your options and the alternatives, you'll be more likely to recognize any emotional influences and either acknowledge and ignore them or consciously incorporate them into your decision.

Decisions may be for better or for worse, and they may be forever, but no matter what, we cannot escape the need to make them and the consequences we reap when we do.

As many lottery winners discovered, the decisions they made after making the decision to buy a lottery ticket often resulted in a lot of good things—paying off debt, going on a long, extravagant vacation, buying a new house, or a new car, getting a new life and new friends. But, their decisions about how they spent the money, and who they gave money to, or didn't give it to, also resulted in suicide, depression, loss of friends and family, distrust of people, and loneliness and greed from those around them.

Whether we win the lottery, land the job of our dreams, grow the business we've always wanted, etc., it's the power and satisfaction we experience when we learn how to make wise decisions that take us where we want to go.

It's fine to make those emotional spur-of-the-moment decisions—to quit your job and join a friend's startup, or buy a lottery ticket, or get married, or fall in love—if you're willing to accept the potential consequences of those decisions. But it's more important to take time to examine your decisions and their consequences as much as possible to get a better gauge of the quality of your decision-making.

What career path should I pursue? What additional studies should I take on to improve my earning power? And for those leading the growth of their company, what direction should we take our company in? All these decisions have an emotional component—fear, excitement, apprehension, doubt. I'm not saying don't feel your feelings. I'm saying acknowledge them and incorporate them into your decision-making process—something that's easier to do with the WINX process.

None of us can foresee the future, but by looking at and considering the alternatives, defining the right challenges, and listening, researching, and defining the right problem to be solved, we can change the world or our corner of it. Not making the right decisions can be catastrophic, especially given a chance to do so.

The WINX 8-Step Process

Everyone wants to win. Winning, succeeding, doing well, learning, and moving forward releases endorphins and it feels good. And since you purchased this book, I assume you want to win big or, as I put it, win *exponentially* where the win is not only good for us but also those around us—our family, spouse, children, company, team, community, and so on.

WINX is a process that helps us win with and because of others. First, let's define winning. For example, *winning is setting and meeting personal or company goals.*

How we define a win does not matter. When you finish reading this book, I hope you define your WIN much bigger. Some people define wins by the number on a scoreboard, a financial gain, a bank account, property, cars, and so on. Others define winning by fame and notoriety, a medal, or their name in the record books.

What you win isn't as important as actually being able to *clearly define **what winning means to you**—*not to your neighbor, boss, or friends. Define your win to make the smart decisions needed to achieve it. I'll go into this more in "defining the problem" in Step 1.

Other things may happen as a result of your *defined win*—but it's the specific win you have in mind that creates the foundation for your decision-making process.

For example, we might think we win based on the parameters we set for ourselves, but what happens when our win results in another person's or group's loss? It could ultimately turn our win into a loss and a long-term loss at that. The important thing to remember is to *assess your goals and take your stakeholders' goals into account as well.* Doing so will help you grow your decision-making skills on an ongoing basis.

WINX is a proven 8-step process that anyone, of any age, experience level, industry, or profession can learn and use after reading this book. It's a process designed to help us personally and professionally. It's meant to help our employees, our clients and customers, and anyone who comes into contact with us along the way.

The more you practice WINX, the better you'll get at making decisions that benefit you and those around you. You will fail at times —usually in the beginning and later down the road as your skills are tested in more complex challenges. The better you get at making good decisions, the more you'll be asked to make more complex decisions—and the learn and fail process will continue. That's how we learn. But ultimately, you will win more and make better decisions.

One caveat: There are no absolute 100 percent guarantees in life with anything, anyone, or any process. WINX won't eliminate all your mistakes or all your bad decisions. It *will help* mitigate, prevent, and ensure that the decisions you do make are the most likely to be the winning decision for you. WINX also helps ensure you're making decisions about the actual problem, not the assumed one.

One of the biggest mistakes people make when making decisions, as you'll soon see, is defining the wrong problem or opportunity. They overlook or ignore the golden nugget to seize the seemingly obvious. That's why a conscious decision-making process keeps both the big picture and the details in front of you at all times—helping ensure you don't miss critical details.

Decisions, Decisions, Decisions

Decisions have an impact, for good or bad, intended or unintended, whether we see their immediate impact or not. Our critical and not-so-critical decisions don't just solve a problem. They're more far-reaching than that. Decisions don't operate in a vacuum, and they're rarely a "one-and-done" thing. They create ripples, and ripples impact the things and people they touch.

Our decisions are part of a larger ecosystem, whether it's our family, company, business, or community. Our decisions, large or small, can and do alter the landscape of the lives of others. That said, we're not responsible for what we can't control. We are responsible for the things and decisions we *can* control and for the actions we take or don't take after our decisions hit the fan or not.

That decision you made at fourteen or sixteen to start smoking cigarettes may or may not come back to haunt you as lung cancer in twenty years. Those forty years you've spent drinking soda and sweet tea may manifest as diabetes in your old age, resulting in limb amputation, blindness, or death—if only you'd made the right decision back then.

The guy or gal you had a crush on and never asked out may confess their never-ending crush on you at a high school reunion twenty years later.

This isn't meant to paralyze you and keep you from making decisions. After all, "no decision" is a decision too. So, if we can't control all aspects of our decisions, how can we make the right decisions? How can we ensure we're not creating more problems than solving them? How can we consistently make good decisions?

The greatest deterrent to making good decisions is making the right decisions about the wrong thing—in other words, not defining or addressing the correct problem. By defining the right problem, we not only make better decisions, right decisions, and efficient decisions, we resolve issues before they become bigger problems.

Not Recognizing the Right Problem

I remember a story from a client who shared it with me. Apparently, the company cafeteria was located above a shop floor where someone decided the machinery below the kitchen posed a "fire hazard." After spending hundreds of thousands of dollars moving the heavy, expensive machinery and experiencing over a week of downtime and lost productivity, one of the welders asked, "Why didn't they just move the kitchen?"

I can't vouch for the story's accuracy. Still, I've heard similar stories about expensive and complex "solutions" that came about due to the wrong problem/challenge being defined or the wrong questions asked. For example, when The Americans with Disabilities Act was first enacted, employers were tasked with providing reasonable accommodations for the disabled. I read the story of one company that completely remodeled an office for a woman who had a disability with one of her arms.

When this employee returned to work and looked at a large amount of remodeling her employer had undertaken to accommodate her disability, she quietly suggested they could have accomplished the same result by simply moving her computer and phone to a different location on her desk!

So what do the above examples teach us? For the WINX process to work, you must take time to define the right issue or problem. Whether it's a problem or an opportunity, ask first, "How can we ensure we are looking at the right thing?"

Start by not rushing the definition of your problem. Have those impacted by the "obvious" weighed in on what they see as the real issue?

The "obvious" issue for one company was that the machinery kept breaking down, needing extra maintenance and care. After asking "why?" enough times, the team leader learned the equipment they had wasn't designed to be used in the way they were using it. At the time it was purchased it worked, but it wasn't meant to be a long-term solution. The downtime and other issues disappeared once the company sold the old equipment and replaced it with newer equipment designed to manufacture the goods they produced.

Rather than "finding a way to maintain the equipment that was always breaking down," the true problem to solve was "finding the correct equipment to do the job."

By involving the machine operators in brainstorming solutions (further explained later in this book), they learned the history of the machine and why it kept breaking down. By not going through the problem-solving process alone, you're less likely to miss a critical aspect of your challenge.

As brilliant, experienced, and savvy as you may be, there are certain decisions you should not make alone. You may be the final word after being presented with different scenarios. Still, in general, you should not make major decisions without the input of your staff, team, or significant others.

It's one thing to decide whether or not to start exercising. You clear it with your doctor and set up a plan. It's quite another to make hiring, firing, moving, or branding decisions without input and careful research from a team. Why do I bring this up? Because your network, your team, and those around you—the people you interact with regularly, will often be the very people you call on for help in making decisions. You need to trust them, work with them, and listen to their input. And as stakeholders, they should be considered in the decision-making process.

One of the essential questions I ask myself when working on a specific problem is: *who else should I interact with to get input on the problem statement process?* When it's time to sit down and look at the thing you need to solve or the challenge you need to address, you don't want to be surrounded by 'yes' men or women. Choose others who don't see things exactly as you do and are willing to speak up and say so.

Acquire as many different points of view from diverse individuals who will help you identify the thing you're defining. To this end, consider these steps:

- Invite colleagues from other industries to participate when you can.
- Talk. Connect. Listen!
- Include your employees—the people on the frontline, customer service reps, receptionists, front of house and back of the house, or any impacted group in creating your problem statement. They're the people who see the most common complaints and questions. They're your front-line people. They often know of or see issues and solutions you never will.
- Research other companies and how they identified similar problems.
- Search online for solutions to see what new technology or approaches have been made. Always be open to learning about advancements and research in your field. Just because you love the mousetrap you've been using doesn't mean someone else hasn't invented a better one. This may change your problem entirely.

Discover

When I go into a corporation, I want to meet the executives and C-suite staff. But eventually, I also want to talk to the line staff, administrative people, and folks at all levels of the company, vendors, and customers where possible. They can often explain how things work when executives don't know. It gives me a chance to pull them into a situation if, where, and when needed.

A colleague once told me he got his best information from the vendors who supplied his client. He happened to be visiting the docks on a company tour when a delivery truck came in. He struck up a conversation with the vendor waiting for his truck to be unloaded. He learned more in those thirty minutes, he told me, than he'd known in three days with the company's executives.

If you've ever been friends with an administrative person, you know that they often know more about the business and what's going on than many others in the organization. However, they're not going to give up that information lightly or for no reason. They must like you, trust you, and see that their input will help, not hurt their position at the company before they talk to you. Never slight, ignore, or disrespect anyone at any level when you work with people. You never know what they have to offer, who they know, or what power they wield.

If you're an entrepreneur, chances are you started off working with anyone who paid you. As business improved and you got more clients, you may have noticed not all those clients were people or companies you wanted to work with, for whatever reason—personal, professional, ethical, financially stable, or not, etc. What mattered was you got the job, and you got paid. The "problem" you were solving was usually "income" related.

I met Susan, a small business owner, at a pre-COVID conference. She was very successful (in her words) but utterly frustrated and ready to give up on her consulting business. She told me it just wasn't worth what she had to put up with to make the money she was making.

"This industry is full of so many jerks!" she said, frustrated. "How do I deal with them, so they don't drive me crazy?" Like many of us, Susan was trying to solve the **wrong problem**—i.e., how to work with her bad clients. I suggested, "Why not redefine the question and uncover the real problem?"

"Which is?" she asked.

"How can I attract better clients, sell my services to them, and eliminate the jerks?"

She was stunned. It had never occurred to her to get rid of her bad client base and find better clients. Like many freelancers and small businesses, she thought she was "stuck" with bad clients because:

1. They were already clients,
2. she needed the income, and,
3. firing clients wasn't an option. She also feared losing the clients who made up half of her client base and were paying her bills.

Serial entrepreneur, freelancer, and business author, Seth Godin, writes about this same turning point in his life in a blog post about "Unreasonable Clients:"[18]

"One of the largest turning points of my career was *firing* the client who accounted for a third of my company's work. We were becoming really good at tolerating the stress that came from this engagement, and it became clear to me that we were about to sign up for a lifetime of clients like that,"[19] he wrote.

The fears Godin had about firing his client and losing that income were real, but he said the ultimate wake-up call for him was realizing that firing this client was the best decision he'd ever made. He didn't try to solve the problem of how to work for these abusive folks. He solved the problem of how to get rid of the clients he didn't want to work with, and how to get the clients he did want to work with. Defining the problem accurately is 90 percent of finding a solution.

"Set free to work for those that we believed deserved our best work, we replaced the lost business in less than six months," he wrote.[20]

I shared his blog post with Susan and we set about defining the real problem she faced—how to attract desirable, likable, deserving clients she wanted to work with, who respected her and what she had to offer and were happy to pay her rates. We worked on identifying her "ideal client," right down to the personality types, financial issues, and how they communicated with her. Did they respect her, her boundaries, and her policies? Did they value what she brought to the table?

Thinking about her soon-to-be new, respectful, better-paying clients was much more exciting than dwelling on negative thoughts like, "How do I work with these jerk clients who drive me crazy?" Thinking about anything having to do with her bad clients sucked the life out of her. But thinking about how to attract her ideal clients energized her.

No, it's not easy to find these clients. I'm learning more and more about how to locate these people. Do you find yourself working with many "difficult clients or customers," the low-paying clients, the clients who don't have the resources, time, energy, or motivation to show up and do the work with you? How many of you assume that who you "should" work with is anyone who just shows up and pays you?

I went through the same process at first as well. It taught me the value of defining the real problem or spotting the real opportunity—and not assuming the challenge you have in front of you is the real challenge/problem that needs to be addressed.

Sometimes defining the real problem, not just the one that seems to be the issue, is difficult. Some clients have insisted, "But this *is* the real problem!" After leading them through a few fact-finding sessions and brainstorming alternatives, many were shocked to realize that what they thought was the real problem, was merely a symptom of the true problem. Many had failed to identify the true problem because they were in a hurry to "solve something" to keep their bosses or stockholders happy.

As I move through the eight WINX process steps with clients, I rely heavily on a "collective brain" approach—the belief that our societies and social networks act as collective brains. Together, we are repositories for information, innovation, and complex designs and awareness. We may not consciously have the solution, but as a group, we have the information and solutions from other challenges to formulate a solution for this challenge. The more diverse the group, the bigger the brainpower.

As a group, we are able to selectively transmit and learn information, outside of our conscious awareness. As Connair Russell and Michael Muthukrishna write, "Innovations occur when previously isolated ideas meet."[21]

For instance, the Industrial Revolution began when the previously isolated ideas of agriculture and technology met. Of course, it's more complex than that, but the convergence of technology and agriculture was indeed the spark that lit the global fire we call the "Industrial Revolution."

According to Barron's, before the 18th century, farmers simply walked along, flinging handfuls of seeds as they went. It was a very inefficient system. Seed distribution was random and uneven. Birds tended to eat most of the seeds that simply lay on the ground. But in

1701, Jethro Tull introduced the seed drill (technology), which planted seeds at the correct depth and in regular rows. The results were dramatic, with a seeds-planted-to-seeds-harvested ratio up to nine times higher than "broadcasting" the seed randomly.[22]

Technology not only impacted the stock market and banking but growing and harvest seasons. "Innovations are where isolated ideas meet," was the order of the day, and it still is. But isolated ideas don't just randomly run into each other. They happen when diversity happens—when people from different industries, in different niches come together and explore solutions—in other words, they connect.

The Harvard Business Review (HBR), has even covered this phenomenon, writing that:

> *"Over the course of years of studying innovation, we've found that there's great power in bringing together people who work in fields that are different from one another yet that are analogous on a deep structural level."*[23]

Bringing in ideas from other industries inspires radical innovation. Bringing in ideas from a diverse population of employees and staff inspires a richer, more creative exchange of ideas. In fact, diversity of race, ethnicity, and gender have been proven to result in greater creativity and insights in solving all kinds of issues.[24]

Richard Freeman, a Harvard economics professor, conducted a study on diversity in science. He discovered that published scientific research gains greater attention if the authors are ethnically diverse. Even diversity in career and work fields makes a difference.

"When you're working on a problem and you pool insights from non-analogous areas, you're likely to get significantly greater novelty in the proposed solutions, for two reasons: People versed in non-analogous fields can draw on different pools of knowledge, and they're not mentally constrained by existing, "known" solutions to the problem in the target field. The greater the distance between the problem and the analogous field, the greater the novelty of the solutions."[25]

For example, 3M developed a breakthrough concept for preventing infections associated with surgery over a decade ago. The experts they consulted weren't doctors, surgeons, or anyone in the medical field. They went to a theatrical-makeup specialist who was knowledgeable about preventing facial skin infections that occurred when applying makeup.[26]

Heinz ketchup sales began to drop in the '70s because people got tired of trying to get their product out of its iconic glass bottle without spraying ketchup everywhere. So, Heinz turned to another industry using different bottling methods for their product—the shampoo industry. In 2002 Heinz created an inverted ketchup bottle with a unique cap that kept the ketchup from leaking out but allowed users easy access to dispensing the product. Sales began to climb again.

If you don't believe networking or connecting with others matters when it comes to making decisions—you must not be a history buff. Another bit of decision-making wisdom—sometimes the best person for the job is someone you loathe, but is someone who can get the job done. Don't let your affection, or lack thereof, influence your decision.

When Good Decisions Lead to Bad Consequences

I know that our life, business, reputation, and happiness come from our decisions in everything we do. Our decisions, especially the ethics we stand by behind those choices, have outcomes that ripple through our world. Those decisions affect everyone involved and make an impact whether we see it or not. Our decisions have a compounding effect, like a pebble skipping across a pond, making rippling waves that touch others in ways we may never know. If knowing how to make better decisions were possible, wouldn't you want to know how to make them?

Unintended Consequences

Long term or short term, even if we personally win, no business or personal decision is effective when others lose. Bad and good decisions can lead to unexpected results with unintended consequences—consequences that change our entire landscape positively or negatively. What you initially thought was a win could quickly turn into a loss—and unfortunately, that happens frequently.

Many companies (and governments) make choices, hoping to solve fundamental or financial problems while not considering the bigger picture. In doing so, they create new problems and more complex challenges. Some make decisions fully aware of the impact those decisions will have on their customers, but don't care. For them, profit takes precedence over everything, even people's lives.

When Ford Motor Company introduced the Ford Pinto to combat the loss of sales to a foreign car market in 1970, Ford knew that the Pinto represented a serious and deadly fire hazard. When struck from the rear, even in low-speed collisions of 20 mph, the gasoline tanks tended to explode, often trapping or killing the vehicle's passengers inside the car and burning them alive.[27] [28]

According to *Moral Issues in Business 8th ed.* [Shaw & Barry (pp. 83–86)] "Ford officials faced an ethical decision. Should they go ahead with the existing design, thereby meeting their production timetable but possibly jeopardizing consumer safety? Or should they delay production of the Pinto by redesigning the gas tank to make it safer and thus concede another year of subcompact dominance to foreign companies?"

To most of us, the answer, certainly an emotional one as well as a seemingly rational one, is obvious—fix the design and delay production. Save lives, not profits. But that's not what happened. Ford not only ignored the obvious path, but they also pushed ahead with the original design and then stuck to it for the next six years, years they could have been retrofitting the vehicles even as people were dying horrible, tragic deaths, burning alive in their vehicles. Why did Ford ignore the emotional side of this tragedy? Because it was less expensive to pay off the lawsuits they would encounter from survivors and families of victims than it would cost to fix the design flaws of the car and to delay bringing it to market.

Ford Motor Company's decision was totally one of cost-benefit reasoning (cost-benefit being a newish term flaunted)—an analysis in monetary terms of the expected costs and benefits of doing something. The human factor, the impact of their decision on the lives of Pinto owners involved in accidents that ended in fatalities and injuries, was not a significant consideration. The term stunned the nation, even the world, and left many people in shock.

Safety improvements to the Pinto would have only cost them $10–$15 in parts and labor per vehicle—a total cost of $137 million to the company. In what would later come to haunt them, the now-infamous term "cost-benefit analysis" was introduced into the public arena—justifying to executives the cost of making a profit versus the cost of protecting human lives. Profit won in the beginning, but their decision would haunt Ford to this day.[29]

According to a variety of case studies and news reports, it wasn't the cost of retrofitting the cars that was considered too expensive. It was the redesign and retooling for the gas tank. That would have delayed Ford's production of the only car that could compete with a foreign market. Therefore, the production delay would have delayed sales of the Pinto for almost two years. This would have cost them millions in lost sales to Japanese car manufacturers. Thus, Ford evidently reasoned that the increased cost in the event of accidents and deaths of Pinto owners outweighed the benefits of a new tank design.[30]

Within four months, Ford sold over 100,000 Pintos. It became one of the company's best-selling cars, dominating the domestic subcompact market. During the model's entire run, from 1971 to 1980, Ford sold over 3.1 million Pintos. It was a great success. Until it wasn't.[31]

The short-term win for Ford—sales and profits—became a long-term loss to both the brand and the company and the more than twenty-seven victims and their friends and families.[32] The losses weren't just financial. They were personal and very emotional. It wasn't "just" three girls killed in a rear-end collision on a Ford Motors spreadsheet.

They were two sisters, Lyn (16) and Judy Ulrich (18), and their cousin Donna Ulrich (18) who were on their way to a church volleyball practice in their five-year-old Ford Pinto on August 10, 1978.

They had just filled up the Pinto's gas tank, when Judy Ulrich, who was driving, noticed she hadn't put the gas cap back on the car. She pulled off the road, put on her hazard lights, and hoped the gas cap hadn't fallen off the trunk. Before she could get out of the car, a van behind them hit the Pinto at full speed.

Richard Dugger, the van's driver, had leaned over to pick up a cigarette he dropped on the floor of his van. He didn't notice the car ahead of him had stopped. He hit the back of Ulrich's Pinto at full speed. As Dugger ran to check on them—the Pinto exploded into fire. Dugger was unable to do anything as the girls burned alive inside, one of them banging helplessly on the window for help as she burned. Two of the girls were killed instantly, the third died later at a local hospital.[33] Ford's spreadsheet and cost analysis didn't show that—at least not to the public—until the case went to court.

The Ulrich explosion would be one of more than two dozen accidents where occupants were either burned alive or were burned over 90 percent of their bodies and survived to sue Ford Motors and win—although at what cost to them and their families?

It's easy to criticize Ford Motors for their seemingly callous and unethical decision, but the fact is, Ford was focused on themselves—like many of us often are—and their decision made perfect sense in a world where profits and losses, not people's lives, ruled. They were able to convince themselves that what they were doing was "okay."

This is more proof that what initially seems to be a great win for your company can turn into great losses over time and impact the very core of your business. This often results in a swift and significant downturn. These negative turns can seemingly come out of nowhere, but they are real and need to be addressed quickly and effectively. As the old adage goes, "The road to hell is paved with good intentions." However, these seemingly well-paved potholes on the road may also have unintended, and deadly, consequences.

Other decisions are stunningly catastrophic—made by experts who make such decisions daily and often under great political and financial pressure with little consideration for the lives of their employees or the public. Their ethical values take a back seat to political or financial profit pressure.

There aren't too many business decisions you might make that would affect the life and death of people, like the decisions NASA constantly faces, but it's good to understand the process and the factors that play a role in such decisions.

During the space race of the '80s, NASA was under pressure to conform to an aggressive launch schedule to help keep "space exploration" in the public eye. Engineers for Morton Thiokol, NASA contractors, strongly recommended delaying the launch for safety reasons. However, members of the White House were disappointed and very upset about a potential delay that would disappoint the American people.

According to the History Channel, the launch urgency factor was primarily political. "President Ronald Reagan was due to mention

McAuliffe and the Teacher in Space in his State of the Union address on Tuesday night. If the launch were delayed, NASA would miss out on another big public mention [of the agency]. If the agency was going to justify continued spending on the [space] program, *Challenger* had to launch on time."[34]

As a result, White House officials pressured NASA and Morton Thiokol to proceed regardless of any cautions not to, a decision that turned out to have deadly but not entirely unexpected consequences. It was a prime example of what happens when you let outside influencers without the expertise to make such decisions, influence your expert decisions based on their personal or professional agendas.[35]

In 1986, when the planned launch date for the *Challenger* mission arrived, the temperature wasn't ideal. In fact, temperatures were significantly lower than what the rocket was designed to handle, and four engineers said so, loudly and repeatedly. They were ignored.

Even though mechanical engineer, fluid dynamicist, and aerodynamicist Roger Boisjoly—the Project manager of the solid fuel boosters of the Shuttle Program System—strenuously objected to the launch of the space shuttle *Challenger* months before the loss of the spacecraft and its crew in January 1986, his warnings were ignored.[36]

Based on previous flight data, Boisjoly correctly predicted the O-rings on the rocket boosters would fail if the shuttle was launched in cold weather. Allan MacDonald, another Thiokol engineer, also strenuously objected to the launch.

Morton Thiokol's managers decided to launch the shuttle despite the men's warnings. Later investigations into the events would claim there was a "miscommunication" about the warnings, and those interviewed would say they never received such information prior to the launch.

Yet, Mark Maier, who directs a leadership program at Chapman University and produced a documentary about the *Challenger* launch decision, told an NPR reporter that: "[MacDonald] was on site the night before the launch, *refusing to sign off on the launch authorization and continuing to argue against it.*" MacDonald later exposed the cover-up.

Informed or uninformed, the decision to launch was made. Sadly, seconds after the *Challenger* launched, the rocket's O-rings malfunctioned just as the engineers had predicted. The rocket exploded, killing all seven astronauts aboard. Later investigation would determine many of the astronauts were alive when they hit the ocean after the explosion.

The decision to launch had unintended, though not unexpected, consequences for the astronauts, their families, and schoolchildren worldwide who were watching the "first school teacher in space"— Christy McAuliffe—on live television.

Thiokol's decisions directly impacted MacDonald and Boisjoly positively and negatively. Both men were criticized by colleagues and their employer for their opposition to the launch. They both suffered emotionally and psychologically in the wake of the deaths. MacDonald was demoted, but after a congressional investigation, later promoted to vice-president of the company and tasked with redesigning the booster rocket joints that failed during the *Challenger* launch. But there was another good consequence that came out of his decision.

After the disaster, MacDonald traveled around the country, talking to engineering schools, speaking about ethical decision-making, and sticking with data to ensure others didn't make the same decisions Morton Thiokol had.[37]

From space launch disasters to an incredible number of dollars lost from a lack of psychological safety, getting feedback remains a challenge in companies worldwide. From Morton Thiokol's decision to launch an unsafe shuttle to Ford Motor Company's decision to put profits ahead of people, it would seem that feedback is something employees would relish giving—except they don't. They're not stupid.

Not everyone has their strength of character and ethics. Many employees do recognize the ethical decisions they're faced with, but in weighing the consequences of giving feedback, they opt not to protect their careers and families, then suffer afterward from regret at not speaking up. MacDonald and Boisjoly both realized the consequences of giving unwelcome feedback and of objecting to the deadly potential of their employer's decisions, but they spoke up anyway.

Every decision we make impacts others, even when the outcome of our decisions is not as horrific as these. Sometimes, decisions are made that seem to be entirely well-intentioned and effective—until they're not realized. So, it makes sense to do your very best to follow the WINX process. Might it have helped in these cases? No one knows. It sure would not have hurt.

Now that we've seen some of the negative impacts of decision-making, intended and not, how do we turn all our decisions into wins? Even more importantly, how do we win exponentially?

Winning Exponentially (WINX)

Winning Exponentially focuses on creating a process to constantly and continuously implement strategic problem-solving and decision-making. This process helps decision-makers mitigate unintended consequences from impacting companies, their customers, and their employees. It assumes those making the decisions are ethical and moral and desire the best outcomes for their companies, customers, and employees.

Winning Exponentially considers the long-term impact of decisions and how companies can "win" more often and more extensively while also helping others—e.g., all those stakeholders with whom they partner—achieve their goals. Winning Exponentially, or "WINX" for short, is focused on serving others by focusing on a collective gain.

WINX is the simple problem-solving model I created based on proven methods and other decision-making models that will improve you and your organization's decision-making process.

WINX will also help you evaluate options in a manner that exposes your risks and the risks of others associated with that decision.

Throughout this book, I break down a simple problem-solving strategy and provide a model to help you better decide, from all the options you or your team assess, which to execute. Finally, I will provide examples and personal stories from my experiences throughout my journey that show the impact of this process on others and on you!

I believe everyone would benefit from a simple process that helps them make better, or as I call them, WINX decisions.

During my lifelong years in the service industry, I lived by a strategy I never recognized until a peer, Mike, pointed out my ability to focus on collective gain. This showed up in many aspects of my life and work.

When I first started writing this book, my focus was solely on business. Yet, as I worked through the book, met with dozens of consultants, and conducted extensive research, I realized that the WINX strategy works equally well at work in our personal lives.

It works if you are an employee or employer. It works if you are a parent, a spouse, or a teen trying to break away and earn independence in this world. It works if you are the CEO of a billion-dollar company. Why? *Because WINX is about you and those around you—assuming they focus on how everyone can win big, with the right mindset, determination, and process.* Good or bad, decisions will most often come back to you, to us. To our shareholders, or our family. The WINX process starts with thinking about a challenge or problem and looking at possible outcomes of your decision. For instance, who will benefit and who might get hurt by this problem-solving decision? It's a powerful framework for thinking wisely, making sound decisions, and taking strategic actions that result in better consequences and outcomes.

WINX is a proven strategy, a step-by-step model that evaluates the risks and benefits of decision-making options so companies and individuals can make "profitable decisions" by understanding the bigger win. It's a method that helps problem-solvers bring potential solutions to any other decision-makers involved in the process and prepares those impacted by the chosen solution.

WINX is a way to:

- Look at a problem from different angles,
- see possible alternative solutions,
- consider the impact on others, and,
- set a powerful intention: It may seem like an over-amplification; however, you will not get to WINX decisions without having the proper intent and goal. So check your mindset. Make sure you're willing to sincerely and honestly INTEND to work toward finding a solution that best supports a triangular look, for the organization: the customer, the company, and the employees, a.k.a., WINX. That's where it all starts.

WINX helps when you get stuck, find yourself sticking your head in the sand, analysis paralysis, or most likely, simply searching for different ideas.

And remember, the WINX process is about getting you and your team in the habit of considering the impact of your decisions on others. Use what works for you.

My guiding philosophy has always been to look at the role and impact of the customer, the company, and the employees in the problem-solving and decision-making process—not just the "bottom line" of a company's financial decisions.

If you don't think the decisions of employees matter, then consider the impact on your business when employees call in sick, quit without notice, or have to leave to pick up a sick child. And if that wasn't enough, look at the impact the COVID-19 pandemic has had on employees—4.5 million of them who quit their jobs in November 2020, and to the hundreds of thousands, if not millions more expected to quit in 2022. Employees are not only the most expensive capital most service companies have, they're the most difficult to recruit, hire, train, and retain. Employees are major contributors to your profits and worth. Their abilities, knowledge, and experience can't be replaced—at least not without great cost and effort.[38]

As Albert Camus wrote, "Life is the sum of all your choices."

So, I say, let's do our best to make good ones.

Overview Of The Winx Process: An 8-Step Framework to Decision Making

Below is a high-level overview of each of the 8 steps in the WINX Framework.

Step 1: Craft Your Problem Statement

Here's one definition of a problem statement: "A concise description of the problem or issues a project seeks to address. The problem statement pinpoints the current situation, the desired future situation, and any disparities between the two." It's an important communication tool for a couple of reasons:

- It ensures that everyone working on a project is working on the same "problem."
- They know what the problem they need to address is and why the project is important.

- It keeps people focused on the problem and potential solutions.

When we begin to see everything in our lives and work as a challenge to learn from or an opportunity to seize, our approach to "problems" changes.

Step 2: Determine the Root Cause Of The Problem

Your problem statement may be perfect, but be sure it addresses the root cause. For example: "Feeling bad," is just a symptom of deeper health issues—just like almost all problems we face are symptoms of a deeper issue, not the problem itself.

It's all well and good to buy antihistamines to address the *symptoms* of your allergies and eliminate the sniffing, hives, and runny nose problem, but what if you address the real problem—pollen and dust in your environment? What if you get allergy shots, install a better filtration system, or wear a mask outdoors during pollen season to eliminate or reduce the pollen we come in contact with rather than just drug ourselves in response to its reaction?

Most of us understand that a runny nose, sore throat, or watery eyes are often a symptom of allergies, a cold, flu, or other bacterial or viral attacks. We can treat the runny nose and the symptoms of those things, but we're not really affecting the root cause—the allergy or virus or issues themselves.

If you break a bone, chip a tooth, or cut your hand, pain, and bleeding are the symptoms of the injury. The root cause is the bleeding that comes from a break or cut. You can take pain medicine to treat the pain, but until the cut is stitched up, the bone is set, or the tooth repaired, you are merely treating the symptoms.

If your company has a high turnover rate, chances are the root cause or the real problem is a manager or supervisor. Why? Because new studies show 57 percent of people quit jobs because of their boss, not because they hate their job.[1] Further, top leaders typically make the decisions. The tendency at many companies may be to blame HR and focus on finding and hiring "better" employees. However, unless you look at the real reason people are quitting, you won't stop the revolving door. You will waste hundreds of thousands of dollars trying to fix a problem that doesn't exist by focusing on the symptom, not the problem.

By simply identifying the right problem—whether it's a boss who needs to be replaced, wages that need to be increased, work shift times that need to be altered to accommodate parents driving their kids to school, improved processes, the culture changed, or workloads adjusted, you're closer to a solution by examining those potential root causes than assuming bad employees are to blame. Establish the root cause and solve that, and the symptoms (high turnover) will naturally resolve.

NOTE: If your problem statement changed based on this step, you might need to re-write your problem statement. Once your problem statement is on track, you are good to go to Step 3.

Step 3: Evaluate the Impact Of the Current Problem

How, when, what, where, and why is this problem impacting the company?

In this step, you will evaluate the impact this problem has on all of your stakeholders or whoever may be affected by your decision or lack thereof. It can be easy to throw your hands up or stick your head in the sand because of the fear of making further mistakes. That is a dangerous place to land. Evaluating the impact will also help you determine if the problem warrants further focus.

Step 4: Problem Solve

When an unexpectedly brutal snowstorm left a foot of snow and ice on major roads, three employees of a small business were unable to get home safely. None of them wanted to risk the drive, or later, to leave after learning that power outages left most of them without heat in their homes even if they'd managed to get home.

Among the alternatives they came up with for what to do, the company discussed putting employees up in a nearby hotel until roads were cleared (the hotel turned out to be full for the night because of the storm), or buying and bringing in air mattresses and sleeping bags from neighboring sporting goods stores.

Through the problem-solving process, one employee's husband, who had a four-wheel-drive truck and experience driving in snow and ice, was called. He volunteered to transport employees to the owner's house, which was only a mile away. The owner's home still had heat, a guest room, couches, and camping cots where everyone could spend the night, shower, eat, and still be able to work the next day after the roads were plowed. The employees' problem was really finding a warm shelter for the night that didn't involve driving, not figuring out how to get everyone home safely. By defining the problem precisely and then exploring the alternatives, they were able to find a workable solution.

As we work through this section, you will read various stories and learn different options and methods of problem-solving.

Step 5: Evaluate Alternatives

What appears to be a great solution doesn't mean it's the best answer. In this step, you will evaluate the impact of the current problem, vs. the alternative solutions you chose during the problem-solving steps. The evaluation will allow you to assess the impact on each of your shareholders. It allows you to see and assess options to make the best decision or recommendation for a WINX solution! This is where the magic happens. You will find it much easier to identify the best solution once you finish this step. This is the one step that I recommend you use in any type of situation you find yourself in. Make Steps 3 and 5 a daily habit. Teach them to your team and shift your culture one issue, one idea, one problem at a time.

Step 6: The Decision Step

This section provides suggestions for those making decisions and, where appropriate, those supporting the decision-maker. Why? The larger the company or the busier the executive, the chances are business owners won't be involved in the decision-making process unless their expertise is needed or until a team or employee has solutions ready to present to them for a final solution. Here, in this step, presenting a solution to the decision-maker(s) means more than a PowerPoint, memo, or one-pager with bullet points. "Door number one, door number two" isn't always the best way to present a decision-maker with choices. There are many more things to consider, remember, and present when giving the decision-maker choices.

Some executives will expect a decision from you based on your research. Others will request options plus your recommendation. This section helps you lay out your recommendations with as much or as little information as the decision-maker needs to make an informed decision. It also, of course, moves the decision-maker into the decision step.

Step 7: Prepare for Impact

Making a decision involves more than just choosing among alternatives. It means not only factoring in the consequences of your choice, but tearing apart your solutions to find the areas some not involved in the process may see as weak or unreasonable aspects, and to separate the pork/fat from the meat and bones. You've made a great decision. You have analyzed the issues and concerns, now tear those suggestions apart so you can be prepared to explain the pros and cons, the strengths and weaknesses, inside out. Factor in the impact of making the decision—knowing who the decision will impact, who will be involved in implementing it, and the next steps. Your job, or someone else, will need to be the cheerleader to recruit others to support the decision. Remember, you or the team that worked through these steps have gone through many options and analyzed the impact on your stakeholders. Without proper explanations and communication, your choice may be... well, *head-scratchers* for your employees, and customers. If you have followed the WINX steps, you should be in good shape.

Step 8: Implement and Manage the Decision

Implementing and managing a decision means more than just saying, "Okay! Let's choose option 2." It means assigning responsibilities and goals, tracking the decision, the outcome, and following up on the impact of the decision. Once a decision is implemented, a post-decision report that evaluates the success or weakness of the decisions can also be helpful. This step helps you prepare for variables that can change or weren't predictable when the decision was made.

I explain each step in detail below, including some examples and stories from my own experiences, clients, and research, plus tips to help you navigate through each step. If you have not done so yet, I recommend downloading the free fillable forms and documents for this book at www.ParoneGroup.com/WINX.

Step 1: Craft Your Problem Statement

"When I have one week to solve a seemingly impossible problem, I spend six days defining the problem. Then, the solution becomes obvious."

— *Albert Einstein*

When you experience pain, it's common to view that pain, or what seems to be causing it, as a problem that must be solved by making a decision. Most of us grew up solving our problems by asking ourselves, "What's wrong?" then identifying what appeared to be the problem and fixing that thing. We brought that same approach to our work lives. We didn't realize that decision-making on a corporate level (and a personal one) can be more complex because they involve more variables and stakeholders.

Example

When my neighbor decided he needed more trash cans because he was renovating his home, all he had to do was check with the city to see what regulations to follow. Then he bought larger cans and later rented a commercial dumpster until his project was finished.

If he had needed more trash cans at his business, he would do essentially the same thing, but would also consider how the dumpster would impact employee parking, customer access to the building, and whether he needed any kind of signage or media alert to let customers know he was still open for business.

He needed to make more decisions, not just about how many more dumpsters or trash cans he needed, but how that simple decision might impact everyone. He might lose customers who think the business is closing, or irritate employees who then carry that resentment into work and alienate customers. Of course, he's free to ignore all that, and just put in the dumpsters and let the fallout land where it may. It's up to him. What would you do?

See how just making a "simple decision" to solve a "simple problem" can create more problems if your solutions aren't well thought out or you don't solve the right problems?

To help you, there is a tool to structure that decision-making process. It's called the "problem statement."

The first step is to write down the issue in a statement format. Make it inclusive. For example, this trash problem statement could read:

> "How many trash cans are required so that the trash I generate is legally condensed in one location?" Keep the statement simple. Focus on the main issue—how much trash to store in this case.

Note that there might be secondary or related challenges that could complicate things and make a solution confusing. So, instead, focus on the one most significant challenge that needs to be solved first. Once you realize this solution, explore other ideas/options other than the first one that jumps out at you.

As you address the most significant challenge with this specific problem of how many trash receptacles to store, keep all of your stakeholders in mind, answer the question as to what will be the impact on your stakeholders which include your customers, employees, and business.

Next ask auxiliary questions that will help you make better decisions such as:

- Are several small cans better than a dumpster?
- Where should the cans be placed in order to allow the same access for employees and customers?

TIP: To come up with the best solutions to any problem, start with a very clear idea of your goals as a company or individual so you're able to formulate the best problem statement,

Example

Air Time Critical®, a European freight forwarder, calls itself "an emergency freight specialist." Their company goals, values, and company culture are very simple and clearly stated on their website:

"Our added value resides in our ability to cut delivery times and provide our manufacturing customers with a turnkey service from pickup to delivery, including paperwork and administration."

So, when an equipment manufacturer based in Tours, France, contacted Air Time Critical® a little before 11 a.m. with a challenge it was facing, Air Time Critical® crafted a very simple problem statement:

To deliver 200kg of automotive spare parts by 3 p.m. at the latest. Now the equipment pallet was ready, but a road express delivery would only get there by 5 p.m.—two hours too late.

Solution: The client requested a dedicated air charter, but ATC® recommended a helicopter delivery instead. Why? The helicopter approach was faster to implement, better able to meet deadlines, and even better, was nearly 2,000 euros cheaper than the air charter.

Given the emergency of the situation, and other factors, the door-to-door helicopter delivery solution wasn't the assumed solution, but it was the best way to go. The client confirmed the agreement at 11:15 a.m. ATC® disassembled the helicopter seats in the helicopter and loaded the automotive goods in parcels so as to fill up the entire available space. Fast forward one hour: the helicopter was on its way to the destination.

Result: With a top speed of 250 (kilometers per hour) km/h, the chartered helicopter's flight only took 2.5 hrs. ATC® delivered the parts to the site at 2:45 p.m.—just in time with minutes to spare."[1]

What stands out about this company is its commitment to optimizing each transport stage in its solution:

The company is specific about what it can deliver.

- It promises customers it can "shave 1 to 3 days off the average door-to-door delivery time frame of express courier services for international air freight."[2]
- The company knows what a "win" looks like and it makes decisions with that in mind.

After you've written your problem statement, have others look at it or read it to them. Get feedback. If there are questions, doubts, or confusion, reword it. You want it specific and accurate. Clarity is crucial and keeping your, or your company's goals in mind is also critical. Other problems that may arise should be added to a separate open items list and treated as open items to address later. Otherwise, you can get bogged down trying to solve each little obstacle as it appears. I work with open item lists with clients when we are organizing their days, weeks, and future planning. That is a bigger topic, but for now, simply know that keeping a separate list of items you want to go back to as your schedule dictates helps you stay focused on the task at hand.

The hardest part of beginning the decision-making process is defining the challenge you're trying to solve. Believe it or not, most people and organizations simply point out "the problem," without stopping to consider if it is indeed truly "the" problem.

Too many of us are willing to speed toward solutions, any solutions. Once we think we have the problem defined, we jump to solve it. We're often afraid that if we spend too much time *defining* the problem rather than *solving* it, we will anger our supervisors, or experience "paralysis through analysis."

Once you understand just how to define a problem, you'll begin to enjoy crafting problem statements because it reduces the size and threat of the problem by defining it because it creates parameters you can work with.

Many times, accomplishing or resolving a problem is nothing more than the art of asking the right questions at the right time, or seeing a solution where others haven't. This is often why outsiders can come into an industry and spot novel or creative solutions immediately— they're not part of the "group think" of the industry. They don't know "how it's always been done." They don't have baggage to unpack around novel solutions either.

When working on solving a problem in the security industry years ago, a new employee—with absolutely no experience in the industry —identified the best solution to a problem. He actually stopped me in my tracks. Everyone in the room was amazed. He clarified the problem in a clear statement, which actually helped us quickly identify the solution. We all get 'stuck' and rooted in our expertise.

Clearly, an outside perspective can bring light to a deep-rooted problem, or even articulating the problem statement!

We limit ourselves to the obvious. We make knee-jerk, on-the-fly, this-is-how-we've-done-it-in-the-past decisions based on feelings, not facts, projections, not data, and urgency, not expediency.

We eliminate the creative, the unexpected, or the alternative approach. We ask: "How do we get a new account or contract?" rather than, "What feature or offering does our product/service have that will benefit the most people, and who are those people?"

We ask: "How can we earn the revenue or income we desire?" rather than "How can we improve productivity or employee satisfaction?"

We ask: "How can we expand the company's business?" rather than "How can we satisfy our employees and customers best to move the company forward?"

Try Changing Your Problem Statement

I'm reminded of an example a colleague shared with me about a problem-solving exercise at one of his client's companies.

The project teams were divided up into small groups and assigned the task of getting a Ping-Pong ball out of a series of tubes using only straws, chopsticks, string, and other small items found on the table. The leader gave each group a "problem statement" about removing the ball from the tube.

An engineer in one of the groups sat back in his chair, sipped from his bottle of water, ate his donut, and quietly watched as his team struggled to devise a tool to remove the ball from the objects on the table.

After finishing his donut, he stood up, leaned over the table, and poured the rest of his bottle of water into the tube. The Ping-Pong ball immediately floated to the top of the tube where he plucked it out of the tube and laid it on the table. Problem solved.

The first response from his team was cheers—and then doubt. "Can we do that? Is that allowed? Is that a real solution?" The initial response was joy, the secondary response was doubt and fear—that the team had done something wrong or something that was not allowed.

Because the solution was different, unexpected, and not within the typical range of possibilities they'd been given, they doubted the success of the move, even though it worked. When the facilitator asked him how he came up with the idea, he said, "I changed the problem statement from 'how to remove the ball from the tube,' to 'how to get the ball to rise to the top so we could easily remove it.'" By ensuring we're asking the right questions, and solving the right problem, we can often open up doors and solutions we didn't know we had.

Let's take a simple example—the vacuum cleaner. For decades, since its original invention in 1901, vacuum cleaners relied on vacuum bags to collect dust and dirt. These bags quickly became clogged with dust and eventually lost suction. Initially, the problem seemed to be *how to design a bag that didn't get clogged.* In fact, many frustrated vacuum-cleaner owners tried many different kinds of vacuum bags, hoping to find the "best" or "right" bag to solve the problem. Their focus was on an "uncloggable" filter.

James Dyson, an inventor, and artist, also became frustrated when his top-of-the-line vacuum cleaner lost suction and failed to clean as well as it once did. He disassembled the vacuum cleaner and discovered that a clogged vacuum bag appeared to be the problem. He had no more luck than the rest of us at resolving the diminished suction issues or the clogged bag issue.

Then one day Dyson was at a local sawmill. He noticed how the sawdust at the mill was being removed from the air by large industrial cyclones—without the use of bags or filters of any kind. The process relied on "cyclonic separation," a process that removes dust and dirt from the air through centrifugal force rather than through filtration as most vacuum cleaners do.

His creative instinct kicked in and he wondered, "could that work on a smaller scale, like for a vacuum cleaner?" It was the beginning of his reframing of the problem. The problem wasn't about the filter—it was about removing dust and dirt from the floor. The filter was one alternative, but Dyson had another.

Dyson told *Guardian* reporter Andrew Dickson that he created a cardboard prototype of a cyclonic separator and strapped it onto his Hoover. "It didn't look great, but it picked up more dust. Fifteen years and more than 5,000 prototypes later, I had a bagless vacuum cleaner," he said.[3]

By defining the problem as "how to remove dust and dirt from the air," rather than "how to create a better vacuum cleaner bag," Dyson revolutionized the vacuum cleaning industry. He went on to invent a wheelbarrow that used a revolving ball rather than the standard wheel to make it easier to transport heavy loads in a wheelbarrow over rough, muddy, and rocky ground. He not only "reinvented the wheel," with his new "ball barrow," he made the "wheel" better.[4]

Dyson's success, like that of many inventors, comes from properly defining the real problem, not the apparent or "obvious" one. Something as simple as seeing the problem differently than hundreds had done before he gave Dyson the opening to a solution that addressed the problem, not the symptom.

There are many companies, coaches, and methods for defining the right problem, and most of them use some or all of the tips I'm about to share. Depending on the industry you're in, and the problem you're trying to solve, some will be helpful, some not so much. If not, leave them and move on to the questions that you can currently answer.

As Karl Popper, one of the most influential 20th-century philosophers of science, once said, "All life is problem-solving." The sooner we realize, acknowledge, and accept that premise, the easier (and more fun) decision-making becomes.

One of the best comments I read when researching the topic for this book came from Glenn Llopis in an article he wrote for *Forbes*. He wrote, "The best leaders are the best problem solvers." He went on to describe the necessary patience it takes to view problems through a broader lens... one of opportunity.

He surmised that leaders without this wisdom tackle problems with linear vision—only seeing the problem right in front of them while obscuring any possibilities the problem may contain.

Tips for Defining the Problem:

- **Don't be fooled by large amounts of data unless it is easily understood and leads to a clear conclusion that matters.** I know many companies invest millions of dollars in collecting and categorizing data. But data alone is useless. It must be analyzed and interpreted to be of any use in solving any challenge. If you're going to use data in defining your challenge, spend more time analyzing it than you do collecting it, and don't rely on it just because it's data. Rely on the analysis, not the numbers.[5] Don't be lulled into the obvious or assume things about the data.

Malcolm Gladwell has honed this ability to see data differently. In his book Outliers, Gladwell turns data—the birthdays of hockey players —into a story that explains why boys with birthdays farther away from the cutoff date tend to be more successful than other players. In an interview with ESPN, he explains:

"It's a beautiful example of a self-fulfilling prophecy. In Canada, the eligibility cutoff for age-class hockey programs is Jan. 1."

Gladwell went on to talk about how seriously Canada takes hockey; therefore, coaches begin funneling the best players into elite programs, where they practice more and play more games and get better coaching, as early as eight or nine. He goes on to ask how do you define the "best" player at age eight? Naturally, the oldest—the kids born nearest the cut-off date, who can be as much as almost a year older than kids born at the other end of that date. At age eight, ten, or eleven more months of maturity is significant. So those kids get special attention. That's why there are more players in the NHL born in January and February and March than in any other month.

He goes on to state that European soccer and American baseball have the same pattern, even to a more extreme degree. He concluded, "It's one of those bizarre, little-remarked-upon facts of professional sports. They're biased against kids with the wrong birthday." The data about these patterns have existed for a long time, but only Gladwell was able to spot the pattern, make sense of it, and craft it into a story that had meaning and impact. The same concept around giving meaning and a story to data in professional baseball formed the basis for the hit movie *Moneyball.* Data alone is worthless. Data that tells a story is powerful.

You will find more information on data in the problem-solving step in this book.

- **Dive Deeper.** The scope of any challenge is rarely obvious. Like icebergs, the mass of the issue tends to lie beneath the surface, and out of view. Don't jump on your first impression. Be skeptical and curious. Look deeper.

- **Ask "Why?" a lot.** Don't be satisfied with one or two "whys." Keep asking until you've exhausted the answers and look closely at those answers to get a different perspective on the issue and challenge before you. For instance, "Maintenance costs on this machine are too expensive." WHY? "It takes too much grease." WHY? "Because it wasn't really designed to do what we're doing with it." WHY? "Because we needed something and this was all we could find at the time." WHY? "Because we were in a rush." WHY? "We needed to meet production." WHY? "Because we'd lose a customer if we couldn't deliver" ...and so on.

In the long run, the company problem-solving team determined the machine they had to maintain cost more than losing the customer and selling the machine and finding different customers! The problem was ultimately: "Is this machine costing us more than we make by servicing it?" They actually dug deeper, found the right machine, renegotiated the contract, added two more customers, and finally began to turn a profit!

- **Ask: Who should benefit or who most benefits from solving this problem?** Who or what do they think the problem is? Who benefits more if you solve a production problem? The employees or the customer or the company? How does each benefit? Who needs to benefit the most and why? Don't be afraid to ask these questions. The answers may not only surprise you, but they may also hold the solution to the problem. Look at all angles and players—there are no sacred cows in problem-solving.

- **Break down silos.** Innovation doesn't happen in isolation. Invite your whole team to look at and define the problem. Don't just say, "This is the problem." Say, "This is the challenge, how can we improve on what's happening now?" and "How would YOU define what's happening now?" Be open and curious. Keep asking "Why"? Be aware employees, customers, and vendors will almost always see problems differently than you do.

- **Be open-minded.** Open-minded people see beyond the obvious details and the "apparent problem" to the true challenge that lies beneath the surface. Risk is their best friend, not their enemy. They tackle issues head-on and get on with the business of driving growth and innovation. Close-minded employees protect their little corner of the world and make issues and problems more about how the change will affect them and less about how to create an opportunity or solve a problem. Learn to identify these employees and work with them to help them see what you're trying to do.[6]

Oh, if only real life were so neatly and easily packaged in inspiring sound bites as are some of these tips, insights, and even scientific research. But it's not. From my own experience here's a story about an actual problem. I call it "Howard's story."

Howard's Story

In a WINX strategy session, I facilitated a group of Property Managers. One senior manager, I'll call him Howard, told us a story when discussing lessons learned during our "defining the problem" segment. His account of what happened helped us cement the need to ask more questions before taking action.

Here is his story:

When working for his last company, Howard's boss decided to drop by a key account to check in with their client, the chairman of the Board of Directors for a very large homeowners association. After a very brief conversation, it was clear to his boss that their account was in jeopardy of being canceled. Why? Because this client felt their board meetings were a waste of time, that nothing ever got done, and they needed to make a change.

This client only had a few minutes, but he was apparently quite clear. Howard's boss always kept a tablet in his car and made notes after meetings. The boss gathered his leadership team and angrily smacked his note on the conference table. The note read in a heavy black marker, "These board meetings are a waste of time. Nothing ever gets done. Something needs to change!" Understanding that one of the critical responsibilities of a property management company is to organize and facilitate these board meetings, this was a concerning statement. I asked Howard to play this out with the team. Start with how his boss may have written the problem statement.

The first problem statement: Account X is in severe jeopardy and they're considering ending our contract.

"So what happened next?" I asked. Howard's boss demanded the termination of the Property Manager. Just for our understanding, I asked Howard if he agreed with this termination.

Howard told me he did *not* agree because he had not investigated the matter. In fact, he added, "Look, that's why I left that company and joined this one! This was not the only person in that company fired before a thorough review. Ready, Fire, Aim was standard!" Then he continued his story:

After terminating Jim, the Property Manager, Howard spoke with one of their new "rising stars" who agreed to take over the massive account. Howard's boss scheduled a meeting with their client. The plan was to make it a great show of effort. Howard, his boss, and the District Manager who worked directly with the Property Managers, all in attendance. They had a presentation that was well thought out and prepared (so they thought) to inform the client of the changes, introduce the new Property Manager, and discuss the plan. Howard's boss felt ready. He was proud that they had taken the bull by the horns, moved quickly, and, as a result, prove their preparedness to execute their plan and solve the problem! Well, the story soon shifted.

As soon as they started the meeting, "It was like a big pan smacked us in the face," Howard said. The client was furious. He immediately threatened to end the contract. "Jim, that Property Manager you fired? He is the only reason your company has stayed on this long." It was a statement that Howard will never forget.

Practice session. At this point in the story, before you read on, write out the problem, restating it at least three times. What was the real problem Howard was facing?

Did you clarify the problem statement? We did the following to improve Howard's Problem Statement:

- Remove descriptive but unverifiable feeling (subjective) words.
- Add factual/verifiable information.
- Include all known information, but not any solutions.

Here is what the practice team came up with the second time:

The second problem statement: The board president feels that board meetings are a "waste of time" where "nothing ever gets done."

Focusing on facts and removing emotions helps clarify the real problems. Can you identify the difference?

Problem statement #1

"Account X is in severe jeopardy and considering ending our contract."

Problem statement #2

The board president feels that board meetings are a "waste of time" where "nothing ever gets done."

There was no explicit threat to the contract. In Step 2, we'll get back to this and learn what the real problem was.

As you saw with Howard in the above problem, stating the problem requires more than just a quick judgment and immediate action. These things often only perpetuate or worsen the problem. So let's look at his situation again. How could Howard have been more specific?

- The second problem statement—Add factual/verifiable information. Note that we have restructured this problem a little later in this book; write your problem statement and then evaluate how you stuck to accurate/verifiable information.
- You created a cause/effect statement. Once you have documented the problem in a statement format, you are ready to move on to the next step.

Step 2: Determine The Root Cause Of The Problem

Step 1 required a deep dive into your problem. You probably have identified the root cause, but some more complicated problems need this extra step. Now that you have clearly stated your problem, it is vital (and easier) to identify the root cause. All problems start somewhere. Getting to the root eliminates the problem. When practical and applicable, pull together a focused team of people involved or affected by the situation to get their input and experience.

Often, the root cause of a challenge is not so obvious. Drilling down a little can help identify the exact cause that needs attention. As you will read very soon, you don't have to "throw the baby out with the bathwater" to find a working solution if you identify the root cause first.

Lessons Learned

Let's look at the problems described in Step 1 with Howard. First, Howard's boss noted the problem statement as "Account X is in severe jeopardy and is considering terminating our contract." After all, effectively planning and facilitating the Board of Directors meetings is a significant responsibility for the Property Manager.

But Howard's boss failed to step back and identify the root cause. As Howard continued, we learned that the problem was not the Property Manager. It was much more complex.

Later learned, significant contributors to the problem mentioned included actions by the Treasurer and Secretary of the Board. They could not make decisions. Regardless of what the Property Manager did, nothing got done. The votes always went south! Getting rid of Jim wasn't the solution when the problem lay with board members.

"Could the Property Manager have done more internally to get some help with this problem?" I asked. Yes; read on.

After losing the account, the boss researched this issue to learn more.

Howard called Jim, the terminated Property Manager, to hear his side. He learned that they struggled with decisions because the board was fighting with each other, never able or willing to make decisions.

Each time Joe, the Property Manager, asked their boss Jake, the District Manager, for help or advice, Joe was told to "deal with it."

Each time Joe was told the problem at the account was HIS problem to solve. Howard learned later that this was a typical response to his direct reports.

Jim was not the problem—the District Manager was. Jake struggled to make decisions. As a result, his direct reports, as well as the company, suffered accordingly. This reminded me of my own assumptions about the manager I did not terminate when I first started my job as a VP. I will write about that more in Step 3. We all make them! Slow down and ask yourself what you're assuming, what you know to be factual, and what you know to be real—not conjecture, not subjective, not driven by rumors or assumptions. Pretend you're an outsider with no dog in the fight. How can you see something for what it is, not for what it may appear to be?

There were many problems identified. The lines of authority were not clear; the District Manager could not make decisions; the Property Manager did not know where to go for support; the problem was not clearly identified, and the root cause was totally ignored.

Practice here: Rewrite the problem, clearly articulated. Then assess the root cause. Remember, as additional issues arise, add them to an open items list. If you start solving every situation as it arises, you'll never finalize the original project.

There are various methods of identifying the root cause, but this is my favorite: the mind map. Mind maps are available in many forms. You can also find free versions simply by searching "free mind maps." A mind map is a great way to consider everything about the problem with minimal structure. Regardless of the method you choose, the overuse of the word WHY is your friend during these discussions.

As a reminder, you may find various problems or challenges to solve as you go through the process. If you do not already have one, create a problem-solving list. It can be as easy as creating an excel document, titled problem list, or open items list. Add additional issues or problems to this list to keep you from being distracted.

People often get distracted as new problems arise. They might get distracted from the issue they are working on. Therefore, unless the "new problem" is greatly impacted by the actual project problem they are working on, they should simply note the new problem so they don't forget it.

Also ask, "Does this make sense?"

As for the lowest hanging fruit, it's great to tackle small quick fixes, but don't get into the trap of working on various issues (a bunch of little things) and not focus like a laser on the real thing that needs resolving.

Another company wasted a lot of time and effort trying to get their welders "up to speed" and working faster so that production wasn't delayed—which was assumed to be the problem because that's where units were backing up.

Production crews were frustrated because they didn't understand why welding teams were being blamed for the slowdown when many argued that the "real" issue was with assembly two stations down from welding. A lack of communication between teams only added to the confusion and frustration.

Finally, the owner of the company assembled a team of workers, one from each of the five stations. They each spent the entire day—on a weekend when the line wasn't running—walking through each stage of the production process with an actual set, and reporting on what they found. It took the team less than two hours to figure out where the real choke point was. It took another three hours, after a company-catered lunch, to come up with a solution—to swap out the stages of the production process, moving the welding and assembly to the last stage, not the middle of the process.

Once everyone had been through the process and worked at each station, they had a better idea of what others did, and they understood what was happening. They were able to identify the real issue and offer practical, simple solutions. Not only was it exciting to see everyone working together to identify the real issue, but it was rewarding to see how they all pulled together to rearrange the assembly line once they figured out how best to set it up.

The playset orders, which were backlogged, took about ten days to catch up on and for the company to fulfill their orders. Rearranging the assembly line was a matter of moving welding stations and took only a weekend to change. The difference, the owner explained, "was like night and day." The choke point was gone. The frustration was gone, and the product was of high or better quality because the teams weren't rushing.

Sometimes the "problem" can be putting the wrong person in a job (the Peter Principle) or reacting to what's attracting people's attention, not what's causing the problem.

It's the rigor or attention that a company puts into defining the problem that ensures whether or not the challenge is solved. But it's important to ensure you don't rush the process. As Stefan Thomke and Donald Reinertsen have noted in an article in the *HBR*, "Organizational teams speed toward a solution, fearing that if they spend too much time defining the problem, their superiors will punish them for taking so long to get to the starting line."[1]

The idea of "rushing the process" reminds me a lot of the man crawling around on his knees under a street light. A police officer watches him for a few minutes, then strolls over and asks him what he's doing. The man replies, "Looking for my keys." The officer gets down on one knee and starts looking, too. Finally, he asks the man, "Are you sure this is where you lost them?" The man says, "Oh no. Not at all. The light's just better here." Don't waste your time working on solutions for the wrong problem or the symptom. Take time to ask questions, and to explore what seems to be the problem and what could be the problem.

Step 3: Evaluate The Impact Of The Current Problem

"Take the time to be deliberate, but when the time for action has arrived, take action and go in."

— Napoleon Bonaparte

It is extremely easy to *not* decide. Often, people who get "stuck" simply don't make a change because they worry things might get worse. Or are afraid of the unknown. But what they forget is that not making a decision is a decision. When going through this model, you will be asked to document the impact of the current problem, side by side with the impact of the various options. And that in itself will help you push forward.

Here is an example. When working with employers, I never recommend terminating anyone if we can help those employees succeed—and often we can. However, when it is clear that we can't, it's time to cut the losses. I can't tell you how often these employers hold on to people until they are so very frustrated because they create such huge problems (and they always do) that the tremendous negative impacts on their customers, often other employees, and always their company, is no longer tolerable.

And I do understand. I had the same problem as a VP. My boss strongly recommended when I started in this role that I replace one of my managers. Of course, thinking I could fix the problem, I held on. I tried and tried to work with him. He was hard-working, loyal, and kind. The problem was, he was not meant for the role of a leader. I will never forget the day I lost a large account over my decision to hold on to this employee for far too long. My poor decision to hold on only got worse. Terminating this man was a difficult task, but it was necessary, and waiting did not help me, my customers, or my employer. (In case you care to know, he is doing great now. He is in a business more suited for him, and yes, we remain friends!)

There are many problems that must be looked at thoroughly when assessing the impact of the current problem.

While researching this book, I read an article by a Navy SEAL that said, "... if there's one thing you learn in Navy SEAL training, it's that decisions don't just randomly or haphazardly happen. You have to make a conscious choice to be someone who makes decisions. You have to "decide to decide."64

Every choice, every decision a SEAL makes has consequences—often life or death consequences—and that's why SEAL training is primarily concerned with a careful, highly structured decision-making process.

One of the misconceptions many people have about the SEALS and other special forces groups, or law enforcement, SWAT teams, etc., is that they're "big risk-takers." They're not. They're among some of the most "risk-averse" people I know. They make careful, calculated decisions—not random, off the cuff, "let's see what happens if we do X" decisions.

Special forces, military men and women, law enforcement, athletes, firefighters, and other first responders—people who spend their lives "taking risks" are more prepared than most and survive incredible things that would kill you or me. How do they manage?

These men don't just learn how to make decisions under pressure, with no sleep, and in the face of imminent threats. They learn how, when, and why to make decisions so the most important decisions can be made next. They make decisions during their training that they'll have to make in the real event. They learn how to make what I call "WINX decisions—decisions that take into account the big picture, the impact of their decisions, the impact on their people, their mission, and their purpose, and how to predict (as much as humanly possible) how far and in what direction the ripples will reach."

"Deciding to decide" isn't an ethos exclusive to the SEALS. Many corporations, leaders, CEOs, and athletes also embrace the term. The best embrace the lifestyle, taking time to research, explore, and examine all their options—just like a SEAL would do.

Founders and owners of a "home office supply" company (let's call them Jim and Gerry), were thrilled after being on several local and national talk shows, podcasts, and blogs. Their niche was entrepreneurs and freelancers, or people working part-time out of a home office—bookkeepers, virtual assistants, and the like. They supplied customers with a variety of unique, creative, and functional home office products, and a colorful and fun alternative to traditional office supplies.

However, thanks to the COVID pandemic, and a new "work at home" workforce in almost every industry, their carefully planned pre-pandemic campaign expanded their social media presence faster than planned.

What they were experiencing is frequently called "The Oprah Effect," a reference to the boost in sales that often follows an influencer's endorsement of a product or service.

Oprah, the queen of powerful influencers, often turned many fashion and lifestyle products into multimillion-dollar companies with a one-time endorsement—which, unfortunately, regularly overwhelmed the company's ability to fulfill demand. Although Jim and Gerry never appeared on Oprah, they still experienced the effects of other powerful influencers who promoted their products.

Shortly after their social media attention increased, Jim and Gerry began to see the demand for their products increase. That was great—until COVID-19 and other events hit. Millions of employees found themselves forced to work during a global lockdown.

This new "work from home" market brought in more demand for their home office products than they could have ever imagined. It was the best of times and the worst of times as the demand for their products coupled with supply chain issues began to impact their ability to provide the quality they were known for. At this point, they initially thought they needed to hire and train more people—a short-term and dicey decision—given the virus and lockdown mandates. They wisely decided not to react to what appeared to be their primary problem without doing more research. What they found was what one could expect:

Their small sales department was experiencing an increase in demand for demos of their software, and shipping was experiencing delays and complaints about product fulfillment. Salespeople began helping the warehouse and customer service began taking on sales in an attempt to stem the demands.

What this company was experiencing was a common phenomenon in all businesses—all the stakeholders (employees, the company, and its customers) had different problems arising from the same issue, in this case—an expanded marketplace presence.

While a jump in sales was great for the company because sales and profits increased, that same jump was also a stressor for employees in shipping and customer service. They were unable to keep up with the increased demand in their departments and felt frustrated.

Customers were both thrilled and disappointed. They wanted the home office products but not all of them received their orders in a timely manner—leading to negative reviews on social media. The positive social media presence they'd had began to diminish as they struggled to find a solution to the demand they'd created.

They had been prepared for more demand when they initially expanded their social media campaign, but they hadn't prepared for the pandemic and the increase in the new work-at-home economy. The perfect storm—"exposure, demand, and unexpected consequences of a global pandemic"—hit in full force, threatening to take them down.

The owner and sales team wanted the increased revenue, but were losing on the other end. Bad revenue ends in bad endings! What if they keep selling, and the "word" on social media trashes the company?

Only by understanding the complete situation and how it impacts all shareholders can you come up with a solution and make wise decisions. Before you take any action, evaluating the impact of a problem involves a focus on:

- Your customers
- Your employees
- Your company

Once you evaluate the potential impact on those stakeholders, can you see a way to a decision that includes a ripple effect you may or may not be able to control? Following the WINX model will help you avoid such problems.

Step 4: Problem-Solving

Let's see if this conjures up a memory or two for you. You were brought into your quarterly top leadership meeting knowing the agenda. This memory starts with you staying up the night before, tossing and turning, wondering if the next termination was you. You can barely eat breakfast. You pick up some freshly brewed coffee on your way to the meeting and sit at the conference table with your peers. No friendly smiles, just uncomfortable greetings. Your boss enters the room and throws the Key Performance Indicators (KPIs) up on the screen. KPIs are the metrics deemed most important by companies. These include revenue growth, profit margins, operating expenses, client retention, and so on.

"Another month of poor sales. The only thing we are excelling at is the rate of lost business." He spends thirty minutes degrading you, possibly yelling and screaming with threats of probable terminations in the near future. "If you can't fix this, I will find someone who can!"

You go back to your division, assemble your managers, and as much as you hate doing this, it's all you know. A repeat of your boss. You might not yell and scream, yet there are murmurs of threats. They slip out of your mouth. You are not as bad off as some of the other divisions. The bar in your particular area is not really declining, yet it never moves. Well, except turnover, and that is going in the wrong direction. The pressure is unbearable. There must be a better way. You want to leave but you have worked for years building vacation time and your home is nearby. So maybe you stay—and keep going in circles.

We all get stuck at times and in this section, you will learn a variety of ideas to move you forward, regardless of your role. Einstein taught us long ago that doing the same thing over and over is insanity, yet so many of us do just that. So how do we solve this? How do we move that bar in a positive direction? What do we do when we don't know what to do? And what happens if we decide to *not* decide?

Problem-solving happens when you identify needed areas of improvement and focus on systematic ways to improve them. At the risk of providing too much information (yikes) let's get deeper into the reasons this book is important, including various ideas that may help with problem-solving and ultimate decision making.

Let's start with data.

I know, I know—one of the cautionary remarks I wrote in the step on identifying the problem was to be cautious of large amounts of data—but I also clarified that the right data easily understood can lead to a clear conclusion that matters.

The right data is golden in both identifying problems and then working toward solutions.

I learned a tremendous number of lessons in data work from my last boss, Len. When I first started working for Len, I was a little concerned that he was suffering from "analysis paralysis." Len provided data routinely, on schedule, and with passion. But as I soon learned, Len was right on target. You see, I was well accustomed to KPIs.

A glance at your KPIs offers an easy way to see where you have been and where you are today. However, these are lagging numbers. And although lagging indicators provide important information, you can't use these numbers to shift results moving forward. Len expressed the need for adding leading indicators.

For example, a lagging indicator may be the number of safety incidents—important in many industries. The way to change the outcome, however, is to identify leading indicators and measure the actions that will move the numbers forward. Some actions that will help improve the numbers for safety incidents might include the percent of employees wearing safety helmets, the number of safety meetings, and so on. All leading indicators. Carefully identifying your leading indicators, such as in my safety example, will help you move the bar and ultimately make an impact on your KPIs.

Now let's take that first memory in this step and see some of the tweaks in Len's company meetings. Yes, he had the KPIs on the screen, but those numbers were accompanied by the leading indicators that helped every region and branch know where we were, and where to focus to move the bar. We celebrated successes and knew what areas to improve. No yelling required. Of course, that does not mean that managers were not replaced. It did, however, give everyone the data needed to improve in time to make a difference.

The Far-Reaching Impact of Decisions

At every level of an organization, every person makes decisions every day, as do our clients and employees. Unfortunately, many of those decisions, although having the appearance of insignificance, produce decidedly significant and unintended consequences.

Good or bad consequences can significantly impact the customer, the company, or the employees.

What if you and every member of your organization understood this? What if every person at every level of the organization learned the far-reaching impact of their decisions?

Further, what if all of this was clarified for employees? What if you could show them how changing their strategies and decision-making process would help them be happier, more productive, and improve success in their personal goals? What if your company and its employees decided to play well together, resulting in improved customer and employee retention and a positive bottom-line impact?

That is the power of WINX. An improved desire and focus at every level of the organization to find better solutions for the customers, the employees, and the company. WINX. Three parties, three wins. Very powerful!

It has a far-reaching impact. Decisions can have positive or negative outcomes affecting many people—beyond our immediate awareness and those closest to us. The far-reaching implications can create more problems than the original problem. Emily is a good example.

Emily's Story

One of my employees assigned to a customer location in Tampa (we'll call her Emily) posed a huge and complex problem. Emily had worked at our Tampa branch for a long time, and her name kept surfacing as a problem. "She is killing us with our client," I was told. "She always blames our company to cover up her mistakes."

When I pushed the issue to learn why they kept holding onto Emily, I heard this: "We can't terminate Emily because if we do, the client will cancel our account." This seemed counterintuitive. Hmmmmm.

I asked for a personal conversation with Emily. I love working with challenging employees and turning lemons into lemonade. And at this point, I needed to assess this problem myself!

Before I met with Emily, I wanted to know as much as possible about her history with the company, what happened, when it started happening, and why it hadn't been addressed so far. The story was Emily was moved from account to account because of the same problem—she worked against the company.

"So why is she still there?" I asked.

"The clients loved her, so it's been next to impossible to pull her out," I was told.

"So why did you reassign her to another account?" I asked.

"Because she knows the business and could get a new account up and running." So, not only did they put her at another client location—it was a more significant account—but also, they made her a front-line supervisor. Then, of course, she did it again. She became close to the client and threw the company under the bus.

Why did she seem to hate the company? Why did they not resolve the issue? What they tried to do to resolve the issue only led to more unanswered questions. I spent almost two hours with Emily at a bookstore while enjoying great coffee and a very gooey, yummy cinnamon roll that took over our sense of smell.

After we laughed at the weight we would probably gain from this meeting and got to know each other a little, we got into the details of the situation. I learned Emily did not hate her company; she hated her supervisor.

But we all know that to Emily, her supervisor WAS the company. She didn't know the owner of her company. She knew her supervisors and the branch administrative assistant that hired her. That's it. So, what happened? The supervisor was disrespectful to Emily. When she called him to resolve problems, he did not follow up with her or address the problems. At some point, Emily assumed that her supervisor didn't care about her or her clients, so she took control. "My company gave me no support, so all I could do was reach out to my client."

You see, when the client called her boss, *then* he responded. "Ahhhh," she thought. "Now I understand how to fix the problems."

Peeling that onion more, we checked on the other employees that reported to the same supervisor and found he treated them the same... The other issue was that they had a sharp but young employee (Emily) who needed guidance.

Let's look at the decisions and the far-reaching impact.

The supervisor was unhappy with Emily. He did nothing to fix his problem with her. It hurt him, his company, his client, Emily, and the other employees at the location. Emily was unhappy with the company (supervisor) and failed to resolve problems professionally. She was hurt, spread poison, and disappointed the client in the company.

The Branch Manager knew of the ongoing problems with Emily, even though they decided not to investigate.

That decision was also one that had a far-reaching impact on their company, employees, and customers—not just the employees and clients that Emily worked with, but the others that this managing supervisor oversaw.

Redefining What It Means to Win

Emily was a great employee, but a poorly aware one. She did her job well but failed to understand how to address the aspects and personalities she encountered from her supervisor. Yes, she spoke poorly about her supervisor to her client—a poor decision that nearly caused her to lose her job. Yet Emily was a hard worker; she cared greatly about customer service and performed her duties to the highest degree. What she did not see was the far-reaching impact of *her decisions about how to get her supervisor's attention.*

After working with Emily, we showed her how to redefine winning. She learned that winning is not only about the customer, but how she could better help her company and her customer by making better decisions. She also learned of the poisonous role she played with the rest of her employees. Finally, we spoke about how she could have handled her supervisor, and although he should have been the leader —titles are secondary to leading.

As we peeled it, I explained: The onion came to the layer of how Emily spoke with her supervisor when he failed to follow up. Emily was angry, threatening, and probably intimidating to him. It was an internal war that expanded to others. Her actions and decisions, and his, had far-reaching impacts.

We developed a plan to help our team with Emily. We helped her understand that companies look for problem-solvers, not "eruptions."

I asked how she would handle this again. She said something like:

"I learned a lot. I would ask for a meeting and sit down (instead of yelling) so that I could calmly explain the situation we were in." Before that, she shared, "I would blame him for everything. Now I see we all need support from others. So I would have asked him what I could do to support him with his follow-up or if it was helpful for me to make any calls for him. And I would have said that if I did not hear back, I would remind him, as I know how busy he is."

"Awesome," I said. "And what if that does not work?"

Emily replied, "Then I'll go to his boss or resign. But I have better tools now to get things done through others rather than bulldozing my way through what frustrates me."

She recognized her actions hurt the customer, the company, and her reputation. I was so excited to hear that Emily had climbed the ladder. According to the manager, she turned from one of their worst employees to one of their best by simply learning and redefining what it means to win and understanding the long-term impact of her decisions.

Oh, and if you are curious, her supervisor was transferred to an administrative position, as he was clearly in the wrong role. And now he is in the right one. A win for all! I know there is not always a role for someone misplaced. Unfortunately, difficult decisions must be made at that time because keeping the person in the wrong role hurts everyone. All you can do is look at the bigger impact. How is that person impacting the customer, the employees, and the company? It makes your decision much clearer.

The Danger of the Single Story

A retired police officer I know once told me if anything ever happened to me, or that I was witness to, if there was a conflict or argument in a parking lot, or a grocery store, or a traffic accident, etc., that it was important I call the police and report the incident immediately. She urged me to try to be the first one to call the police.

Confused and curious, I asked why. She shrugged and said, "Just like school and the playground, the person who tells her story first tends to be the person the cops believe, even if it's a lie. If they hear the other person's story first, they will have a tendency to believe it more than yours, even if you're the one in the right. And, it's not uncommon to have the other party call in and lie about events, which makes you look like the guilty party. It's not fair, it's not right, but it's human nature."

I've heard various versions of the same advice from other professionals about the tendency to believe the first version of a story we hear. Even when we know there are two (or more) sides to everything, we still have a tendency to give the first story more credibility, just as we have a dangerous tendency to act on "the single story."

We (as human beings) have other tendencies too—like believing our image of someone or something based on stereotypes, or media representations. When we see images and stories of gangs killing and robbing villages in Mexico, or crime anywhere in the world, we tend to think the entire country is like that. If other countries only saw rioting in Washington state, or forest fires in California on the news every night, they might think all of America was rioting or burning. We tend to hold on to images we see in the media or believe stories we heard about other races or people while growing up. And, we believe the single story.

"The problem with stereotypes is not that they are untrue, but that they are incomplete," novelist Chimamanda Ngozi Adichie said during her 2009 Global TED talk. Adichie was speaking on "the danger of a single story."[1] The timing of the talk couldn't have been more powerful. For a few years during my career, I was a Regional Labor Relations Manager. It felt like she was speaking directly to me during this talk because as soon as I heard her, a light went off. I have been speaking to clients about her talk ever since. It's not only a powerful reminder to be fair and hear all sides of a story, but to avoid stereotypes, assumptions, and preconceptions. It's a call to be aware that you may act on things in good faith, but blindly—not knowing what you don't know.

This is a caution as to how acting without all the information and facts around an incident can cause you to make inaccurate, biased, and wrong decisions based on incomplete evidence. It's a warning to not let your decisions be clouded by assumptions, your personal background, or your work history. Or even what you hear from others. As noted from the story of Emily above, the Branch Manager was acting on information that was not all the full detail.

Our limiting beliefs can come from how we were raised or who we live with, who we connect with, or any combination of these things. That is why as parents we worry about our children's friends. Who are they? Do they take drugs? Will they influence my children?

The danger of a single story happens every day in ways we're not even aware of. If you live in the US and get involved in politics, you will find it difficult to get the straight story on the news. For that reason, I watch both conservative and liberal news shows (which, by the way, drives my husband crazy.) There is so much bias I find it nearly impossible to piece together the full story without hearing all sides of the issue. Often, I chuckle when one news station shares a quote of a president or past president that is correct except for one thing—they omit the rest of the sentence.

In fact, I watched a speech myself and noticed how only half of a story on a particular issue was shared later by the media. Some stations do not cover full topics that the public should understand. I have found liberal bias, conservative bias, corporate bias, activist/cause bias, and more. So even when you get facts, they may be half-truths. Someone said, "Beware of half-truths; you may get the wrong half."

The single-story, half-truths, omissions, and additions are sometimes intentional, and often unintentional. I heard it from XYZ, so I assume it is so. This story illustrates that, as decision-makers, we should understand that we often don't know what we don't know.

For a WINX outcome, we need to open our thoughts to, not only *our side of issues* but just as importantly, "the other side" of them—or facts—looking for the things we don't know.

This is something lawyers are taught in law school and then spend years perfecting after they have graduated. This exercise of looking at and then *practicing* arguing for one side and then the other develops one's ability to go deeper to better understand and better articulate the powerful arguments on each side of a decision. It involves researching both (all) sides and examining each side as though it was our only position.

Robin Eichert[2] is a consultant and founder of PeopleSense Consulting. In her blog, she writes about the dangers of making decisions based on a single story. She gives the example of an employee coming to a manager to complain about another employee.

After hearing the story, this manager wants to take action immediately and confront and discipline the employee. However, as someone once told her, "There are two sides to every story, and some truth in both." The manager's job is to set aside her own tendency to want to act immediately. You need to pause, investigate, and understand both (all) perspectives and create a solution based on both (all) stories, not just one.

She points out that if you act without all the information, you send a message that one person's opinion is valued more than anyone else's. As a result, you may pursue an inappropriate or wrong solution, punish or discipline an innocent person, or be dragged into an employee drama you aren't/weren't aware of. Or worse yet, your solution may backfire and result in legal ramifications or other litigious actions.

I am constantly amazed at how supervisors assume things about what happened, who was involved, and why things happened when they actually had very little knowledge about the event, who was involved, or why they might have happened to begin with.

I'm not alone. In looking back at my assumptions about the steel mills and the unions, I remember the employees and union representatives did the same thing—relying on their one story, not both sides of the story.

As mentioned above, look at US politics. If you are a Republican and watch Fox news, or you're a Democrat and watch MSNBC, you will hear two different stories. Both are half stories. Neither one is the whole truth and nothing but the truth. There is always "more to the story" than what appears in either case. The danger of "one story" isn't limited to work and business. We do it in our personal lives as well.

When we meet someone, within the first seven seconds, people will make what they think is a correct impression of who you are, and you will do the same. However, as a recent *Psychology Today* article points out, through decades of research in social psychology, our inferences are often wrong, and there are "common errors" in our social perceptions.

Other research suggests a tenth of a second is all it takes to start determining traits like trustworthiness.[3] You really don't have time to turn on the charm, name drop, or cover up any blunders you may have made walking up to the person.[4]

I met my husband on Match.com. I'm not all about looks, but the first impression I had of him was made on his appearance. That was one part of the story. I was pleased to learn the rest of the story (who he truly was) was even better. But there can be a real danger in basing a decision on a single story or a single impression.

You're always building trust and creating an impression of who you are with your employees, and your teams. Getting both (all) sides will make your decisions more accurate, but as you teach your team how to hear all sides, consider all sides, and solve conflicts independently, you become a role model for them.

It's very easy to charge ahead when you're in the middle of what appears to be an obvious problem. You think you know the answer or the solution, and you're anxious to fix it, to appear to be in control and a strong leader. But so many things that appear to be "the truth, the whole truth, and nothing but the truth" are not the whole story.

Take the time to get the whole story, or at least as much of all sides as you can.

To be able to do this, the people, employees, customers, and participants you engage with must feel safe.

What is safe? It's *not* "warm and fuzzy." Safe is *not* "nice." It's an environment where, as Amy Edmonson relates in her new book, *The Fearless Organization*, "Individuals feel they can speak up, express their concerns, and be heard."

Edmonson explains that a psychologically safe workplace is "one where people are *not* full of fear, and *not* trying to cover their tracks to avoid being embarrassed or punished." A safe space is not a space where people aren't offended or confronted. It's an environment where, as Edmonson and I, and many leaders advocate, there is candor from leaders—toward and with their employees, clients, and customers.

The workplace and business is more about being open, honest, and filled with candor, even if it means being direct to the point where it makes people uncomfortable.

As a leader, you not only have the right to ask hard questions but a responsibility to. It's up to you to ask, "Is this the right decision? Are we collecting the right data? What impact might this have on others? Are we even asking the right questions?"[5]

When we feel psychologically safe in a relationship, at work, or with customers, we're willing to accept that we can be ignorant about some things and very smart about others, but still willing to explore those blank spots in our experience. Psychologically safe employees and customers are more interested in learning, excellence, and genuinely connecting with others than in looking good or being the best.[6]

The more psychologically safe a culture, workplace, and team is, the more likely your decisions are to be smart decisions that create exponential wins for everyone.

Invite Relevant Stakeholders to Participate in Problem-Solving

Another way to assess and keep your finger on the pulse of what your stakeholders, especially your employees, want is to routinely include them in your problem-solving efforts and decisions through brainstorming.

I can't tell you how often I suggest to leaders that they are not the only ones who can solve problems. From a time-management perspective alone, it makes sense to let others help. And the big benefit? Employees' voices are precious to any manager who wants to make a well-informed decision because they know more than anyone what's really going on, what's truly needed, and "where all the bodies are buried" (meaning where chokepoints and issues are). There is more than one side to every story and the intelligent manager wants to hear those other sides before making decisions. They want to know more about the potential impact and who might be affected. Not knowing "what's on the other side" of an employee or customer experience can lead to a wrong decision.

In a Harvard Business School blog article, Lauren Landry writes about managers involving their teams in decision-making precisely so they can hear all sides and perspectives around their decisions. Landry cites research that shows diversity leads to better decision-making. In addition, bringing people into the discussion from different cultural and disciplinary backgrounds enhances creativity and provides various views on the problem.

There are many benefits to team problem-solving. Without enough research and evaluation, managers often get a consensus ("convergence of ideas") too quickly. The team is valuable when offering individual and independent, often conflicting, ideas. But what if employees are not contributing? Ask what I call soft questions.

- "Susan, you've been quiet today. Do you see a problem with the solution proposed?"
- "Can anyone here shoot down this idea?"
- "What are we forgetting?"
- "What group will be negatively affected if we go forward?"

Team members problem-solving increases employee engagement. The process shows the manager trusts team opinions and judgments. It facilitates collaboration and communication.

Research shows that 75 percent of employers rate teamwork and collaboration as "very important." But 39 percent of employees say their organization doesn't collaborate enough. Other research shows that 86 percent of respondents say workplace failures are due to a lack of collaboration or ineffective communication.

The point is to communicate with your team members. Ask for their opinions, whether they agree with you or not. In fact, the most value comes from those who disagree. They are preparing you for potentially negative fallout or maybe even total failure of your idea. But, at the very least, they will help you bulletproof your plan.

Another benefit of consulting team members is to find your "blind spots." What are your strengths and weaknesses, and how do they impact your decisions? In the *HBR*, Tasha Eurich talks about how important managers' self-awareness is. In her five-year research program, she found that 95 percent of people think they are self-aware, but only 10 to 15 percent are. Team strengths can help correct manager weaknesses.

If you want a WINX team, help your employees understand the power of Winning Exponentially by equally assessing the needs of all stakeholders and avoiding the danger of "the single story" as referenced earlier in this section.

If you listen closely, they and your customers can also help you identify B'RULES. I have been studying Mindvalley for years, where I first heard the term B'RULES. Vishen Lakhiani, the Founder and CEO of Mindvalley, explained that B'RULES are "bullshit rules." They are based on what we think society wants from us, or a rule we established for an outdated reason. A B'RULE is typically easy to identify. Simply, when someone asks why, and no one can give a reasonable explanation, or, the response is "we have always done it that way." Often I have found B'RULES created when someone at the top failed to problem solve, and instead chose to make the easiest or most risk-free decision regardless of its impact on others.

If there's one common thread that runs throughout the entire WINX process, it's that problem solving is a team event. Yes, you may make decisions on your own. I do not agree with decisions by consensus. However, a "team" to research and explore alternatives and collaborate for better ways works. You may actually be the team— relying on experience, the input of colleagues on key points, research, and intuition to make day-to-day decisions. But when it's time to make decisions of impact, it's time to collaborate. More than anything else, collaboration keeps us from focusing on one version of a problem.

Scenario Work

I have watched teams identify brilliant solutions to problems in scenario work. For example, I worked with a small private home supply company on earning customer loyalty. In this meeting, I provided the group with a scenario of a customer being upset because the drill he purchased did not work. The customer was angry. The end of the story was quite fun because the customer had no idea how to use the drill. (Customers are never wrong, right? Belly laugh allowed!!) The challenge was for the group to identify approaches to turn this customer into a raving fan. They struggled at first, then identified an okay solution. I kept pressing. They identified a slightly better idea. Now the manager got excited, and he kept pressing, offering a small gift card for the best solution. He made it fun. It was a small gift, but just enough to get the group excited. They were amazing. At the end of the day, each of them had a solution to an industry problem before they faced it! We also changed the term "problem" to "challenge." Much easier to do when working on preventing rather than reacting!

Look Beyond the Moment

Think about the impact of your decision down the road. Again, I bring up the COVID and hospital staffing example. I bring it up, not because I'm on one side or the other, but because it's an excellent example of a company not looking down the road at the consequences of their decisions in the short term.

Take note if you lay-off, or fire now, for whatever reason, especially in a field as specialized as health care, if you want to keep your doors open and keep serving the same number of people—or more. Making assumptions like, "We'll just get the governor to call in the National Guard to act as nurses," might be a short-term solution, but not a long-term one. There must be other options, popular or not.

I see two common mistakes corporations make in deciding to replace a valuable employee. One, they keep "poisonous" employees too long. These employees often negatively impact the company, customers (or patients in the above case), or other employees if they remain while management looks for a replacement. Even more common is poor leadership—the leader who doesn't help, motivate, support, or hold employees accountable. Very often I have found employees want to do a good job, but need strong leadership.

Even, however, with counseling and help, some employees will not make the necessary changes to justify keeping them. Some you can keep until you find a replacement, but you need to move quickly to do so. By working on your recruiting year-round and staying connected to valuable resources that may have turned down positions or left your company, you won't have poor performers or have openings for long.

Depending on the situation, you sometimes need to cut your losses and fire employees quickly—e.g., avoid legal liabilities, protect your brand, or quell bullying, sexual harassment, or other issues.

Sometimes training or coaching a poorly performing employee helps. Other times it does not. Remember Emily? She was a good employee with a bad supervisor. Today, with 57 percent of employees leaving companies because of poor management or supervisors, you may want to investigate further if the employee is valuable. They may need coaching, a new supervisor, or to be placed in a new department.

The adage, "Hire slow and fire fast," could apply. Companies tell me, "We have to do something now. We can't wait to find and train a replacement." Their discomfort, fear, or frustration is so great that they just want the employee gone. Here, the decision to be made is strictly around their discomfort with the existing employee.

Employee Issues rarely crop up overnight. They almost always involve situations that can be worked on or resolved before a need to act immediately. And they should be addressed as soon as things become an issue to avoid outcomes such as a productivity gap.

Take Dan, a CFO (not his real name), where the death of his young child in an automobile accident, his and his wife's injuries, and the resulting depression, anger, and poor performance that followed weren't unexpected. However, his company was willing to give him time to grieve over his losses as they adjusted to his plunge in performance. What they weren't expecting was how quickly Dan's entire life was spiraling out of control because of the accident.

In the months after the funeral, his wife also filed for a divorce (not uncommon when parents lose a young child). His emotional instability over the loss of his child and then his wife led to an increasing number of mistakes, poor decisions, and a negative impact on the small company he was working for. The owner didn't want to "pile on" extra stress, as he said, and fire him on top of everything else going on in his life, but something had to be done to preserve his business.

With a good severance package, firing Dan immediately seemed the only option. The owner couldn't afford to temporarily hire another person to step in for Dan. He also couldn't afford to lose Dan entirely, as he was a longtime employee that customers and employees truly respected and valued. The owner was upset and frantic to make the best decision for his company, for Dan, and his customers.

While the entire company liked Dan, they could no longer afford to have him underperforming and making the mistakes he was making after a year.

In modeling the WINX process, they concluded that they were willing to give Dan one more chance if he was prepared to work under full-time supervision, give up his title and responsibilities, get psychological counseling, and report to another manager—one who used to be a peer, and one whom Dan trusted. They relieved Dan of his responsibilities to reduce the workload and pressure on him, not punish him. They delegated many of his job duties to other employees, all of whom were ready to take on the extra responsibility while Dan recovered.

Dan was essentially reduced from his former position as a leader and decision-maker to where he only had one responsibility—the number-crunching he was best at. That one skill would be the hardest skill for the company to replace quickly or easily.

The change in Dan was almost immediate. Relieved of the pressure of the responsibilities of his former position, and by seeing a counselor, and working with a supportive manager who held him accountable for specific actions, Dan was able to turn his situation around. It wasn't easy and did not happen overnight.

There were times he came close to failing to keep his promises and his performance up to par, but he managed to do so. Within the 90-day trial period he had agreed to, he had shown enough improvement that he earned another 90-days' grace, then another. Another year passed, and Dan was well on his way to being the employee he had once been. He still had issues, but he was working and stable. His divorce went through quickly, and with counseling, he was able to cope with the many losses he'd experienced and use his work to help him heal.

During this time, the owner also made another smart decision—to cross-train employees in vital areas such as accounting, sales, and IT. He made sure that if another employee were injured, killed, sick, or on maternity leave, a qualified backup or two could step in and take over until a replacement could be hired.

It was a learning experience for all involved. There were many decisions to be made, and most were difficult, but they turned out to be the right ones. Because the decisions were made with careful deliberation and soul searching by the owner and managers, and a variety of alternatives not usually considered were examined, the company did well not to fire Dan.

Some employees turned out to be more gifted and actually performed better in different positions, and all employees became more valuable as a result of the extra training. The owner hired a small IT firm to come in on a part-time basis to familiarize themselves with his company's operation and systems. They streamlined some processes, freeing up IT staff to tend to other projects. Raises were put on hold for a couple of years in exchange for "bonuses" based on performance.

Not every company has the luxury to accommodate employees as Dan's did. The personal approach worked because the company was small, and employees liked and were willing to help Dan and make some sacrifices. I also ensured they consulted with experts to check the legal implications, as these were out-of-the-box solutions that could have otherwise proven to result in high risk. Larger companies with more resources, other decisions, and bigger needs might have fired Dan, given him a severance package, and hired another accountant.

The difference in decisions doesn't mean one company was right and the other was wrong. I am currently working with a landscaping company that has been able to provide support by creating a position for a long time and a loyal vice president who suffered from a serious illness. He is returning in a somewhat limited capacity, moving to a job that will provide the company with his support that will improve service in a needed area, all while helping his replacement. That creates a win-win all the way around. Yes, they added a position. However, they believe the role will help their bottom line in the end.

Based on the company's problem statement, resources, and company culture, all three of these decisions were right for these companies.

CVS also effectively modeled the WINX process when it made a huge decision to take tobacco off its shelves. Their decision didn't change the practices of other companies, yet it was the right decision for them, their brand, and their culture. You can't look to other companies to decide whether your decision is the "right one." It has to be the "best decision" for you and your company. To do anything differently would be like deciding on what college to attend or career to pursue based on what a neighbor has chosen. Things might work out, but would they be in your best interests overall?

How Pivoting Saved Their Business

Remember the office supply company in Step 3? By following the WINX process, this company came up with a creative option—they pivoted. Rather than responding as many business coaches suggested, they turned to authenticity instead. They used their new social media platforms to share with customers what they themselves were experiencing. They used their own struggles to build a connection with customers who were as frustrated as they were with lockdowns and all that came with them.

As a "home office supply" company, they decided they were the experts customers would turn to for guidance in this new "Wild West" of work. They started a podcast and interviewed people working from home. In interviews and podcasts, they explained that they too were scrambling to cope with the "new normal," and to address supply chain issues, fewer employees, etc. They immediately related to their customer base, who were struggling with the same challenges.

They told customers their own home office products were in high demand and short supply and thanked them for their patience, explaining they were committed to not destroying their brand to meet demand. They set an example for small businesses and entrepreneurs about what to do when the unexpected hit.

They turned their blogs into "how-to" content for employees now working at home. They addressed things like how to set work boundaries with families, how to create a home office in a closet, or make their Zoom calls look more professional. Their followers learned that while their office products were indeed awesome, their attitude and their approach to a workplace that changed weekly were more important.

They held free webinars on how to cope with depression, how to deal with babies and toddlers in the "home office" and how to stay healthy, get exercise, and work on communication skills with their spouses or roommates. They shifted the customer focus from "Where are my office products?!" to something they could provide—mental and emotional skills that would prove to be vital in the coming months.

By focusing on the office "products" they *could* provide (content, how-to, and community support online) they created a true, loyal following. Those customers who were there during the tough times trusted them because they were candid and authentic.

Customers were even more supportive of the office products as mandates lifted and supplies became available. Jim and Gerry shifted what could have been a negative experience that broke them and their "company" into a positive outcome with a silver, no wait—with a platinum lining! They had taken their strengths and turned them into opportunities.

In other words, leverage your strengths. And one of your strengths should be to know when to make a decision, and when you need help. Leveraging your strengths isn't a new or untested concept. Wally Byam, the founder of Airstream trailers, started his company during the Great Depression—leveraging his strengths—his love for travel, adventure, and camping. The Gallup Organization created the science of strengths to maximize individual potential.

When you're facing big problems, you will face negative and stressful thoughts. Instead of buying into those thoughts, actively imagine the best possible scenario. As a result, you can find silver linings to replace negative thoughts. As a species, we tend to overestimate risks and presume negative consequences. Learn how to change your thoughts to a proactive rather than reactive mindset. Just don't freeze. Continue to remind yourself that no decision has an impact, too!

When evaluating the impact on your stockholders (employees, customers/clients, and company), don't assume or guess at what they want or how they may be impacted. If you don't know, ask them. You may be shocked and even relieved at how little the other side wants. But, if you assume, or offer something YOU would want, you may not find out what they truly want. We often tend to catastrophize situations and imagine someone wants far more than what they do. Let *them* tell you what would set things right for them.

For instance, when a vendor threatened to end a contract over a "delivery dispute," the dock foreman sat down with the company's representatives and the truck drivers. After some discussion, they discovered all it would take to "make things right" was to change delivery days so the truckers didn't have to wait four to six hours in a nearby parking lot for an hour's slot in which to drop their loads.

By simply changing the delivery dates to another day of the week when there were no other deliveries, these smaller trucks didn't have to sit idle, waiting to unload. The company had been prepared to offer huge discounts and make all sorts of concessions to keep them, but first, they wisely asked, "What can we do to make things right?" All the company wanted was to get their drivers in and out, unloaded, and back on the road as quickly as possible so they were making money and not burning fuel idling in the yard.

The Art of Evaluating Alternatives

Later, in Step 5, we will be evaluating alternatives, but let's start looking into identifying alternatives with a deeper dive into problem-solving.

Beef or chicken? Italian or Chinese? If you've ever had to pick a restaurant with a spouse, or an office full of hungry co-workers with only an hour to "take lunch," you know how much effort a simple decision, like whether to order pizza or go out to eat, takes.

Most of us will instantly factor in things like cost, what employees want or can afford to pay for lunch, and how much time each alternative takes. How long will it take for a takeout order to be prepared, or a pizza to be delivered, versus everyone carpooling or walking to the restaurant of choice? Ultimately, some people will pick one option, and the others will go with another.

Making larger decisions isn't unlike making small ones. Once the challenge has been defined, the options compared and evaluated, and the relevancy to the challenge determined, it's fairly easy to determine the next steps. Everyone wants lunch decisions to go well. It's the same with all decisions in a WINX company. Some decisions take seconds or minutes, while others take weeks or months. Some decisions require all the steps I've outlined, some take only a few. What all decisions have in common, however, is that a WINX company has employees and executives who want the entire company to succeed. That takes making choices at every level from a WINX view. That takes looking from all angles. Choosing next moves that take everyone in the same direction because that's where they want to be! When the entire team builds the WINX culture, choices become easier to make and enforce.

WINX employees are at the front of the organization. As mentioned earlier, they know what makes customers happy and—upset. They know their company—and its products. They know what works, and what doesn't work. They know when to speak up, and when to stay silent. They generally want the company to succeed as much as the C-suite executives and owners. They have the kind of information that is powerful, and they can change the direction of a company if their insights and advice are communicated and followed.

But employees, customers, and vendors will not share their feedback without trust in the people at the top of the company—the type of trust where employees feel safe speaking out. Employees are anxious to share information that can greatly support, or in some cases, make or break the company because they have a vested interest in their jobs/careers. Some will speak out and share information regardless of the company's stance if they feel compelled to do the right thing. These are the whistleblowers and loyal employees whose initial efforts and feedback are often ignored at the company's loss.

Remember Allan McDonald, who directed the booster rocket project at NASA contractor Morton Thiokol? He was responsible for the two massive rockets that would launch the shuttle into space and was at the Kennedy Space Center in Florida for the launch of the *Challenger* "to approve or disapprove a launch if something came up," he told an NPR reporter in 2016.

That interview took place thirty years after the *Challenger* exploded. MacDonald was an employee with a critical decision to make and feedback to give. It was on him whether or not to sign an official form approving the launch, or decline to sign it, stopping or delaying the launch.

He risked the lives of the seven astronauts set to board the spacecraft the next morning. And if he refused to sign, he'd risk losing his job, his career, and the good life he'd built for his wife and four children.

"I made the smartest decision I ever made in my lifetime," McDonald told the reporter. "I refused to sign the form. I just thought we were taking risks we shouldn't be taking."

McDonald wasn't the only employee objecting to the launch. In January 1986, Roger Boisjoly was a booster rocket engineer at NASA contractor Morton Thiokol in Utah. He and four colleagues, including McDonald, strenuously objected to the fatal decision to launch the space shuttle *Challenger*—even explaining in memos six months to a year prior to the *Challenger's* launch—that such a decision could cost the lives of the astronauts on board. "I fought like hell to stop that launch," he told NPR years later.[7]

"I'm very angry that nobody listened," Boisjoly said in his NPR interview.[8] He said he repeatedly asked himself if he could have done anything differently. "We were talking to the right people; the people who had the power to stop that launch." Although his employer, Morton Thiokol, didn't listen, or listened and chose to make the wrong decision anyway, in the years after the disaster Boisjoly traveled around the country speaking to engineering students about the ethics of decisions.

Why? Many reasons. People don't want to be known as a whistleblower, a complainer, or a killer of ideas. Many don't think their boss wants to hear the truth. Some don't think their role warrants giving suggestions or opinions and possibly a beating up by their boss for stepping out of line. Others are afraid of retaliation. Some simply need help in how to make suggestions. The truth is, it's essential to find your "Why." Without front-line views, we lose many tremendous opportunities for creative solutions. So how do we get people to open up, especially if they fear retaliation for doing so?

All the research we reviewed narrowed down to mainly one thing in getting employee buy-in: earning the trust of your employees, staff, team members, and customers.

The Importance of Trust in Feedback

If you want feedback and teams that consistently find solutions to problems, and I hope you do, it's up to you to earn the type of trust that ensures your team that you wish to value, and expect feedback when brainstorming, troubleshooting, or crafting problem statements. Expecting employees to "be there" for you won't work if you're not there for them as well.

A president of a mid-sized organization hired a consulting group when his top leaders recommended he get help on being open to suggestions from his team. Although he did "not agree 100 percent," he hired consultants to help his team in a few areas.

This consulting group called me to partner with them. My job was to dig into the team's motivation and job satisfaction levels. They also asked for help in introducing my WINX program.

I unexpectedly found his team reasonably engaged. They cared about their company. Finally, after understanding the WINX philosophy and looking at problems through the eyes of customers, the company, and the team, they ran with WINX! They were energized to learn the WINX process.

The president was also interested in and learned the eight steps of the WINX process. But he did not want to be a part of the WINX problem-solving process—not because he disagreed with the philosophy, but rather because he believed he did not have time. "That's why I bring these highly educated and skilled executives into the business," he said. "Let's see what they come up with; then, I will decide."

"Fair enough," I said. After all, we were also working on his focus on the top issues the company was facing.

His executive team aced the presented recommendation. Their ability to articulate the impact on the company, customers, and employees was no less than brilliant. I observed the president throughout this process. He showed no emotion. No interest. He asked no questions. His only comment was that he appreciated their work and would decide.

I could see and feel the energy in the room drop. The team entered the room enthused, prepared, and excited to bring forward a great idea to solve a problem. It was not a life-or-death problem that would change the company's outcome if they failed to call it right. It was, however, something that would make a significant impact on the employees. It was pretty simple, yet brilliant.

The president was a very busy man. We all knew that. But he failed to recognize the team's engagement and the time they spent perfecting the solution.

I gave it a couple of days and requested a meeting with the president. We met the next day. He liked the idea, but pushed it aside. He had many more high-level issues to work through. I get that; most people do. But what did that do to his team? How enthused would they be to work on future problems or needs based on his lack of interest?

"How do you feel about their proposal?" I asked. He had a couple of questions, but assumed those concerns were resolved. He planned to give it his approval. Then I wondered how much time he felt it would take to implement. And, if he felt comfortable that his top leader could handle all the work. He said, "Without a doubt."

We discussed the drop in energy in the room and how that might have been avoided. He mentioned it before I did and knew he needed to get back to them. "I'm just so damn busy," he said.

Then, I asked him to assess the impact of taking that "hour or two" out of his day to meet and finalize the project sooner than later.

What impact would taking two hours from his project have on his customers, company, and employees? None, he admitted.

What impact did his lack of sincere appreciation and shared excitement with the team have on his leadership team? He felt they were used to his busy schedule, yet agreed they were clearly demotivated.

And my last question looking long term was, "What impact could it have on your customers, your company, and your employees to continually demotivate your team?"

He decided he had not only demotivated his team, but he might also have stopped them from bringing viable ideas to him moving forward. His avoidance could lead to a long-term lack of psychological safety.

At the end of the day, the president executed a rebound. He shared his delight with the work the team accomplished, apologized for appearing to lack enthusiasm, asked a few questions, worked out a couple of issues, and approved the proposal almost exactly as presented.

When we ask our employees for feedback, it's essential to be interested. Ask questions and express your intent to give it serious consideration. If you can't get back to them right away, make sure they know you are interested and will get back with a fixed date if possible.

Luckily, in this case, the president agreed with the recommendation. But what if he didn't? How do you motivate employees to provide feedback knowing that all of their suggestions can't be implemented?

How To Say No When Employees Give Feedback

Brainstorming and idea generation should be an integral part of your culture. Engaged employees will want to offer feedback as opportunities and/or problems arise.

This is because employee feedback helps break bad habits, reinforces positive behavior, and enables teams to work more effectively toward their goals. Employee feedback can be about anything from the condition of the break room or working conditions to training, performance, skills, or an employee's ability to work within a team. It can be something as simple as parking concerns to safety concerns, culture, pay, benefits, harassment, or how employees are treated. And that can save corporations millions! Yet, very often, when I speak to leaders about employee feedback they hesitate. *Not necessarily because they disagree with the opportunity*, but rather because they know some of their ideas will not work.

So then, how can we solve that problem? It is important to share common goals. That might sound challenging, yet working through this process may be the key to unlocking the magic. How can this problem or solution work in the bigger picture for everyone, at every level of your organization? Consider teaching them WINX. That could be by providing copies of the book, using the forms provided, conducting scenario work, or calling us to help. As a reminder, you can sign up for a self-assessment tool and additional information at www.ParoneGroup.com/WINXassessment. A more specific focus on employees should be available by the time you are reading this book. Bottom line? Get on the same page, looking at issues from all angles. Understanding the bigger picture. Help them do the same.

In the meantime, below are some additional thoughts on the subject, and ideas for how to say no, without discouraging your team. A Gallup study of 469 business units found that managers who received feedback on their strengths showed 8.9 percent greater profitability post-intervention.[9] It's not just managers who benefit from feedback. Employees who are heard and whose input is respected, even if it's not utilized, are more engaged, productive, and loyal as well. To be engaged, employees need to identify with the mission and purpose of the company and they can't do that if they don't have a way to insert their feedback in productive ways.

In spite of all the good things that can come out of feedback, not every piece of feedback you're going to hear is going to be relevant, practical, or valuable. The employee may not have a grasp of the issue or may be offering up feedback to improve her own situation. She may suggest ideas without considering how it affects the company or co-workers. The employee may not realize you have already thought of the idea or tried it and failed. The feedback may be offered in a blaming way rather than a proactive way—complaining without offering solutions. She may not have the best skills, timing, or awareness to offer good feedback.

You may appreciate the feedback, but you won't always have time to go in-depth with an explanation to employees when you need to say "no." You may be distracted, stressed, angry, tired, on your way to or from a meeting, or just not in the mood for feedback. Yet, you need it —even if you choose for whatever reason, to reject it. The challenge is how to structure the feedback process, and how to keep employees engaged and motivated despite their disappointment in hearing you say "no."

"Every word has consequences. Every silence, too."

— Jean-Paul Sartre

Small improvements matter as much as large ones. There are a few appropriate responses when you must say "no" to an employee or customer for their feedback.

Start by showing appreciation for the offer of feedback. A simple "Thanks for taking the time to review and comment," is enough to show you are grateful, even if you are not able to accept or consider the feedback at the time. If they persist over time, it's important to take time to engage with them and encourage them to continue submitting feedback, even though that particular feedback isn't actionable at that time.

It's also helpful to ***explain the situation***. Your team or the person you're speaking with can't read your mind. Your quick rejection might leave them guessing about your "true intent." On the other hand, you don't want to discourage them from giving you feedback in the future. For example, letting them know why you're saying no can help ease the sting, and leave them wanting to keep contributing:

"That's a great idea. I only wish I had that idea sooner, as it's too late to make changes because the document has already been released." Or, "The customer is on his way over, and while your idea has merit, there's not enough time to discuss any additional changes." This will tell your team that the rejection is based on this one situation and that future feedback is still okay.

You may honestly value the feedback, but in the hallway or the parking lot or on your way into a meeting is not the best time to receive it. Instead of saying "no," you can say "not now." You can offer "office hours" or days where feedback is welcomed and employees are invited to make time to discuss their feedback with you. Or, you can ask them to write down their comments and email them, or drop them in an employee suggestion box for you to read later. Or you can plan for a later meeting or some other form of acknowledgment. But you need to do and/or say something appropriate, positive, and encouraging. As humans, we tend to take no answer as a negative response.

As I mentioned, in the section on The Importance of Trust in Feedback, the president didn't acknowledge, respond, or communicate his stance in any way. His blank face and lack of reaction of any kind spoke volumes. He didn't realize he was communicating. And that was the problem I addressed with him. The more people understand your reason for saying "no," the easier your "no" is tolerated. Whether you take an employee's feedback into serious consideration or not, be sure to consider the suggestions and thank them for taking the time to give the feedback.

***Praise or comment on the aspect of the feedback you
can appreciate***, such as: "It's obvious you spent a lot of time and
thought on your idea. I appreciate your hard work and input."

To important people, we take the time to explain "why." Why not do
the same with our staff and employees? If the boss does not take the
time to explain why to them, employees will think the boss thinks
they are unimportant or have nothing to offer—as he did.

> *"If you choose not to deal with an issue, you give up your right of
> control over the issue, and it will select the path of least resistance."*
>
> *— Susan Del Gatto*

***Asking questions may help the employee come to the
same conclusion you have***. For example, if an employee
suggests a change that would make him happy, but negatively impact
the customers or company, ask questions. You might first tell him you
appreciate his idea. Learn how his suggestion may be helpful to him
by asking the "why" questions, but indicate your concerns with
employee impact. Then, suggest that he review the WINX model
and tell you what other ideas he comes up with. Who knows, he may
find a workable idea, or he may learn on his own why his concept
does not work.

It's great to help people understand you value ideas, want them, and
expect them. However, they should also know you can't use every
idea that comes to the table, but that they should keep on trying! You
might also explain that you will take their suggestions under
advisement for a later or more appropriate time. Often, timing is
everything!

Can someone else's good idea make you look bad?
Another interesting comment came out when the president spoke
about his initial reaction. He admitted it was a little difficult to hear

his employees come up with a better idea than the current plan, which he had developed.

That combines a couple of the reasons leaders fail—first, ego. Second, trust in their team for ideas and decisions. If an employee's idea is better than yours and you don't implement it because of ego or resentment, the rest of your employees will know and lose trust in you. And, they'll be much less likely to bring any more suggestions to you in the future.

This president learned a big lesson. Look for reasons to say yes, not no. Celebrate employees' opinions, especially when their ideas are better than yours. And always recognize that these employees cared enough to try. Failure is valuable because those who never fail to step outside of their narrow view or comfort zone stay stuck where they are.

The president also said he realized that the team was smart, skilled, and cared. And that he was proud to be a part of "their" team.

Of course, I jumped in and said that was an impressive lesson in itself! The higher we get in a company, it's more critical to bring in people more innovative than we are. That moves the company forward, freeing you to focus on the higher-level goals.

The energy in that room skyrocketed. The production throughout the company was again rocking.

One final note before saying NO. Take a shower, do a non-related task, and noodle on it just a little more to find a different way to make it work. So this one might shock you, but how often have you literally "figured it out" when least expected? When I take my dog for a walk, when I take a shower, and even when I am doing my aqua aerobics class at the gym, it is amazing how I come up with ideas I struggled to figure out. Then, as I was conducting my final review for this book, I was also taking a class by best-selling author Ron Friedman, PhD who provides science-backed strategies. I should not have been shocked (however I was) to learn there are at least five science-backed reasons that showers help with creativity, like the benefits of diffusing your attention, and a whole lot more. So step away! Forget about it and, according to Dr. Friedman's research, your subconscious mind will keep working for you! Do this whenever you can, throughout each of the WINX steps.

You just might find a WINX way to say YES!

Complement Your Weaknesses with a Strong Team

Some leaders think it's their job to know all the answers. But that simply makes you a know-it-all. Of course, no one knows it all. But you can probably make good decisions if you know where to find answers.

If you want people to be vulnerable and open, take the lead. Let people know you are not perfect. Share mistakes you've made. Discuss poor decisions that led to avoidable problems. Share ideas from those that led to excellent outcomes. Learn how to laugh at yourself.

We grow every time we learn a lesson. Many quotes can be displayed throughout your organization to help your team know you respect ideas and that no one will be fired for a bad idea.

Ever hear the phrase "hire to complement your weaknesses"? We often gravitate toward people who think as we do because it's easier to agree with them and find comfortable, common ground on ideas and problems. But if we want to grow or improve, we need people to push us outside that most comfortable, cozy box in which we hide.

We need to surround ourselves with colleagues who have other messages for us—different messages. Maybe statements that contradict our own. Challenge us in some way. Make us rethink what we've said. That's how we can bullet-proof our decisions and ensure we have the best solution.

"Most decisions are not binary, and there are usually better answers waiting to be found—if you do the analysis and involve the right people."

— Jamie Diamond

To accept different, even opposing messages, managers must be self-confident. They must know they are not being threatened because someone else comes up with a great idea. Maybe a better idea than the manager's idea. The manager doesn't realize that this makes them stronger, not weaker. They will be recognized and appreciated for creating a great team with great views. The confident manager encourages confident team members to voice their opinions and feedback in a safe environment.

Don't Kill the Messenger

Some leaders will ask, "What did you think about _________?" But do they really want to know? If they hear an answer they disagree with, they will often get defensive and start verbally "beating up" the person that gave the opinion.

They only want to listen to the people who think like them and employees know this and avoid being honest with them. As a result, they are unprepared to handle the real issues (they had their head stuck in the sand) which will then come back to bite them in the future.

You need, and hopefully, you will learn to want, honest feedback from people you trust. In business, people earn your trust by taking care of you, listening to you, doing what they promise to do, and giving you their honest opinion, whether you like it or not.

You'll probably go adrift and make mistakes without feedback from trusted friends, teammates, partners, or colleagues. You can quickly lose sight of what's important to them. Their goals. Their values. You will not be aligned with the company's direction. You will offend customers. You need good feedback, even if it hurts.

What Makes a Good Team Participant?

Good, reliable feedback on WINX decisions can come from your team, assuming that team is effective. What makes the team effective? Google conducted a two-year study on 180 teams to answer that question. Called Project Aristotle, the study involved over 200 interviews and evaluated 250 different possible factors. There was no clear conclusion about what constituted the best kind of team, so the researchers started studying the intangibles. That's the point where things began to fall into place.

The Google study group came up with five factors that seemed to be associated with most of the most effective teams:

- Dependability
- Structure/clarity
- Meaning
- Impact
- Psychological safety

Teams with these characteristics make good decisions and provide honest feedback to one another.

Effective team members are dependable—they can be counted on to meet expectations and get things done on time. They know what is expected of them, and they know what the team goals are. From a WINX perspective, if they participate in a decision, they would see if it aligned with the company goals. Additionally, they have a good idea of who would be affected by the decision.

Responsible team members feel their decisions are meaningful and have an impact on the company, as well as on the greater good. And that is the goal of WINX decisions. To have a positive outcome for all.

The fifth factor, psychological safety, is critical to getting feedback that matters. Psychological safety will move a department and a company forward. It will tell managers whether they were right or wrong. To feel safe means team members are confident that whatever they say "won't be used against them."

It sounds like someone reading your Miranda Rights, doesn't it? "Anything you say can be used against you in a court of law." Unfortunately, that is true in many companies. This results in a lack of psychological safety. Employees must be very guarded about what they say in front of colleagues, especially in meetings or in front of management. Saying the wrong thing can jeopardize their jobs and even their careers.

Employees want to be empowered—given power by their managers. That power-sharing allows employees and team members to say whatever is necessary without fear of reprisal. Without being scorned or ridiculed. Without any kind of repercussion.

This is the only way employees, their departments, and companies can be innovative. We need people who think differently, feel free to speak, and say things we disagree with and don't want to hear. Things that may be critical of what we are going to decide. That's the most valuable feedback there is.

And that's the type of people you should hire. Individuals who don't think like you. People who are more intelligent than you and challenge you. People that help you make the right decisions will help you, and your department will rise above everyone else in your company. And that will help your company to thrive and excel.

People are often afraid to speak up and be perceived as wrong. I read a LinkedIn post by Lia Garvin, TED X speaker, and author. Lia recommends not to settle on someone with only an education and job experience. Instead, hire people who are kind, honest, and have a strong work ethic. Perfect, I thought! These are the type of people who would care enough to provide feedback if they feel safe.

I get it. We've all been in meetings and have held back questions or ideas for fear of seeming incompetent. It's unnerving when you feel as though you're in an environment where everything you do or say is under a microscope.

But imagine a different setting. A situation where everyone is safe to take risks, voice their opinions, and ask judgment-free questions. A culture where managers provide air cover and create safe zones so employees can let down their guard. That's psychological safety.

If hesitation still remains, you might consider sending out the agenda in advance, which includes an open discussion on a specific topic for ideas. This would allow participants time to think in advance or even do a little research.

Group Cohesiveness

There is a saying that "there is safety in numbers." That saying works well if a group of teenagers is heading into a haunted house. After the "You go first," "No, you go first," exchanges, someone says, "Let's all go in together." That's group cohesiveness.

In that situation, there is no individual freedom. It works for teenagers when they're scared. But in the business world, it fails. Amy Edmondson of Harvard University wrote a paper titled *Psychological Safety and Learning Behavior in Work Teams*. Her idea of safety is quite different. She says, "I conceptualize learning at the group level of analysis as an ongoing process of reflection and action, characterized by asking questions, seeking feedback, experimenting, reflecting on results, and discussing errors or unexpected outcomes of action." She went on to talk about how, when a team discovers gaps in its plans and makes changes accordingly, team members must test assumptions and discuss differences of opinion openly.

Ms. Edmonson added, "Team psychological safety is defined as a shared belief that the team is safe for interpersonal risk-taking. Team psychological safety is not the same as group cohesiveness, as research has shown that cohesiveness can reduce willingness to disagree and challenge others' views."

In other words, being in a tight-knit group does not necessarily mean members are (psychologically) safe. On the contrary, it might mean the opposite. Members want to "stay tight" and not challenge anything or anyone. Safety means that the members trust each other enough and have sufficient confidence that the team will not punish them for speaking up. Trust has to be at a team level, promoted by each team member, including the team leader.

Team members must feel valued as individuals. There can be no threat of consequences to members who give differing opinions. It is the difference of views that makes teams great. And recognizing this is what makes leaders great.

When I was starting my management career, I was in the nuclear security industry. My then-boss for many years, Jack, taught me so many life lessons in earning trust and developing relationships. Security is a 24-hour day, 7 days per week industry. Jack required that we tour the nuclear power plants on all shifts to get to know our people and understand them. At first, I did this because he required it of me, but it didn't take me long to learn the benefits of these conversations. Soon, these visits were the favorite part of my job. We all had the opportunity to learn about the needs of our most valuable commodity, our employees. And these employees were able to better learn about the needs of our company, and understand their tremendous ability to provide a higher value service our customers deserve. We even worked with the teams to create what we termed our Nuclear Commitment and I remember it to this day:

To Provide a Work Environment of Mutual Dignity, Fairness, and Respect

To Pursue Excellence as Professionals

To Grow Profitably

Under Jack's leadership, I watched what it meant to make a difference, and paid those lessons forward throughout my life. We all need a Jack to learn from. It was not just by listening to Jack I learned. It was by watching him live his talk year after year. Be that person that does right, and considers key stakeholders every step of the way. Lead the way!

"Example is not the main thing in influencing others, it is the only thing."

— Albert Schweitzer

Having a diverse team, and then getting to know each other, helps build the type of trust that it takes to get the critical feedback to make important decisions. Or better understand what went right or wrong and how you can do better next time. So there is strength, not in numbers, but in diversity.

Facing Uncertainty

Umer Zaman and Maha Abbasiiv studied the role of psychological safety and how it affects the ability of employees to face or avoid the uncertainties of change. "Uncertainty avoidance" is feelings of "being fearful of complex, unknown, or uncertain situations" where anything can happen and can't be predicted or controlled.

According to this research, "voice behavior" is less common (employees do not voice their opinions or speak out as much). There is low flexibility in these organizations and less creativity. Employees are less likely to learn on their own or seek more information. They will not challenge the status quo in such environments or take risks.

By creating psychological safety, leaders help their teams learn and grow. They will be stronger. Have better attitudes. They can face the future and be more ready to deal with uncertainty and change. That's what makes a leader a WINX leader. Someone who cares about employees, the company, and customers.

More on Employee Feedback

If you prevent people from providing feedback because you would rather stick your head in the sand, remember—the ocean will continue to roll in no matter what. And what they think remains relevant even if they are wrong. Even if they are negative, it is better to hear and have discussions around negative or different feedback than to have the employees have those conversations with everyone except you!

Feedback is critical, and comments or feedback from employees are often the last wall between making a good decision or a bad one. Remember, it was employees at Samsung whose feedback about the dangerous manufacturing of cell phones could have prevented phones from burning and blowing up. Their feedback was ignored.

NASA? They ignored the feedback from several engineers about the O-rings on the space shuttle that cost the lives of seven astronauts.

The truth is, many companies don't want to hear candid and truthful feedback from their employees. According to a Leadership IQ study, ignoring employee feedback is having a disastrous impact on employee engagement, morale, and culture. [10]

From January–June 2017, Leadership IQ surveyed 27,048 executives, managers, and employees and discovered:

- Just 15 percent of employees believe that their organization always openly shares the challenges facing it. If an employee believes that their company always openly shares the challenges facing it, they're about ten times more likely to recommend it as a great employer.
- Only 24 percent of people say that their leader always encourages and recognizes suggestions for improvement. And if someone thinks their leader constantly encourages and recognizes suggestions for improvement, they're about twelve times more likely to recommend it as a great employer.
- Only 6 percent of people say that at their organization, good suggestions or valid complaints from employees always lead to important changes. If someone says good suggestions or valid complaints from employees always lead to important changes, they're about eighteen times more likely to recommend the company as a great employer.
- Only 23 percent of people say that when they share their work problems with their leader, he/she always responds constructively. And if someone says the leader always responds constructively when they share their work problems, they're about twelve times more likely to recommend the company as a great employer. [11]

The study also showed too few leaders are open to hearing feedback or suggestions. I've seen time and time again that executives don't like to see the rank and file come up with better suggestions than the leadership. They don't realize that's what great leaders value—

employee engagement and concern that benefits the company. This isn't a competition.

When employees of any rank or role have good feedback, it should be examined for the value it brings, not for who came up with the idea. For instance, Richard Montañez was a janitor for Frito-Lay's Rancho Cucamonga plant when he invented Flamin' Hot Cheetos. You'd think executives would have eaten up the idea and heavily invested in it. But they didn't. According to an *LA Times* interview with Montañez, Frito-Lay's corporate backstabbers tried to sabotage him for "stepping out of line." After all, he was "just a janitor." [12]

Montañez, confident in his idea and himself, out-hustled them. Flamin' Hot Cheetos became a hugely popular snack. Janitor or not, Montañez had imagined a chili-covered Cheeto and believed in himself enough to call up the chief executive to pitch his idea. The rest is history. At the time, his position paid $4 an hour. The only way to go was up.

Montañez didn't just stop at inventing the popular snack. According to the *LA Times*, he went on to write a book for Penguin-Random House, and now speaks at different events around the country, including Walmart, Target, Harvard, and USC, commanding from $5,000 to $50,000 per talk.

He was just the janitor. According to *Newsweek* and other news sources, Frito-Lay is making "billions" on the snack—nearly every major Frito-Lay line, from Smartfood popcorn to Funyuns, now has a Flamin' Hot variety on the market. [13] [14]

How can you encourage your employees to come up with creative ideas that bring success to the company and the team as well as other employees and customers?

- Create trust between managers and team members to achieve honest feedback.

- Develop the confidence to hire people more intelligent than themselves.
- Stay open to others with ideas different from yours.
- Develop constant psychological safety for employees to learn and grow.
- Keep your door open to get regular feedback and even complaints from your employees. This way you will remove the development of *surprise complaints* that may reach you too late to address effectively.
- Ask for ideas. You might even have contests. This is a little different from asking for feedback.
- And conduct routine confidential surveys through a third party so there is no risk of identifying the employee's identity.

Surveys

I spend a lot of time working on surveys for my clients because it is here that we gain tremendous knowledge on what matters, where the company is strong, and where it needs to improve.

Ask good questions, measure trends, provide feedback and, of course, follow up. I learned a great method of follow-up from the Gallup Organization during my last job as a Sr. Vice President. Gallup refers to these follow-up meetings with employees as Impact Sessions. It is a great way to share results, and get front-line ideas on solutions. There is no better way to continue to get participation than to show you actually read these surveys and take action. Third-party confidential surveys provide you with information from people who otherwise might not share. With the proper positioning of strategic questions, as well as room for open feedback, they help you take a deeper look into your employees' needs and wants, and even improve service levels.

Still Stuck? Try Brainstorming

In brainstorming sessions, the point is to generate ideas, solutions, and thoughts about all the ways we can approach and solve this problem—with no logic or reason. Have fun with this process. Yell (yep, yell) out ideas that might be great, just okay, or even wild and crazy, and play off other participants' ideas. The goal is to identify as many alternatives as we can, and then, later, we can narrow the list down.

So then why don't we just ask for reasonable ideas? Because some of the craziest ideas have generated ideas outside the norm that have worked beautifully! I have seen it many times. Be sure to have one person who is quick to write the ideas on a grease board and just go! Time the session and request the number of ideas you want. For example, we have twenty minutes to arrive at fifty ideas. At the end of the brainstorming comes more fun! Now, look at this list and start reaching beyond crazy. You can even have a contest for the craziest idea (just for fun) and the craziest idea that resulted in an idea worth considering. Don't worry, we will get to narrowing the list.

In one session, employees had worked hard and had come up with an impressive number of alternatives, but the stress was wearing on them and some were starting to take questions about "their" alternatives personally. "Take a break," I said and watched as the six employees left the room to get something to eat or drink or check their phones. While they were gone, I pulled up a slide of a chessboard. When they came back, I asked them if they'd ever played checkers or chess. All had played checkers, half had played chess, and one employee was actually on his high school chess team.

"What's the number one difference between the two games?" I asked.

"In checkers, all the pieces can move the same, and in chess, each piece can only move a certain way," someone said.

"Chess is more strategic than checkers," another said.

We spent a good ten minutes discussing the pros and cons and the metaphors of both games. What they ultimately realized was that there's a time and place for both games, but that when it came time to evaluate their various solutions and options, they needed to "play chess," look ahead, testing each move against a myriad of possible faults or opportunities.

Later in this process, after you generate numerous ideas, you will metaphorically "play chess"—meaning spending time brainstorming various solutions with a focus on how each solution will uniquely impact your key stakeholders: your customers, your employees, and your company. When you think of an idea, then move ahead—envision it in a different setting, seeing how it will impact each shareholder. Remember, customers have different needs than employees, and sometimes they'll share needs, or have needs in opposition with the company's best interest—for instance, meeting the customer's wants may impact company profits and culture. What solution will satisfy the most needs?

In chess, we look at the possible moves and the consequences of our current move on future moves. Just as each chess piece is different, so are our employees, vendors, customers, and the public. How will each "move" you take empower or impact them?

However, when you brainstorm different options and solutions, your goal is to have a "no judgment" zone where all ideas and thoughts are welcome, and where participants are free to debate (not argue). One of the core tenets of brainstorming—"no criticism"—is misguided. Charlan Nemeth, a professor of psychology at the University of California, Berkeley, found that groups encouraged to debate generated 20 percent more ideas than those told not to critique each other's ideas.[15]

In that space, your goal should be to identify as many solutions as possible for each stakeholder and then discuss your best solutions with your team or internal focus group. or both. Listen and ask questions to understand each person's thoughts thoroughly. Especially consider the ideas of those with whom you disagree. Why? Because the ideas of those with whom you disagree can help you discover any blind spots you may not be aware that you have Following are ways to help you identify solutions:

- Use word associations.
- Tell stories about the situation.
- Look at photos of the problem.
- Focus on the quantity of ideas, not the quality.
- Give yourself boundaries—like asking what solution you'd use if you only had twenty-three or forty-eight hours to implement it.
- Take away boundaries—ask yourself what solution you'd use if money, time, resources, and expertise weren't a problem. For example, I needed support services for my customers that I could not provide. I thought I would hire employees, but since the services needed were not consistent, I struggled to find the best of the best and keep them employed. I changed my strategy and now have a bench of fifteen partners and that number grows as needed. I found my solution by walking away from my initial plan.
- Create diverse teams—bring in employees from different departments, or even host a focus group of outside people. Buy them lunch and pay them for their time.
- Use the 6-5-3 method—where six people generate three ideas in five minutes. This will generate 108 ideas in a half-hour. You need six participants. Give everyone a separate piece of paper and ask them to write down three ideas in five minutes. Next, have them pass their paper to the right. Give them five more minutes to write down another three ideas before passing their papers to the right again. Repeat this process until their own paper comes back to them. Brainstorming can happen anytime. Finally, create a

company folder where employees can add ideas whenever they can.

When I conduct brainstorming sessions, I ask them to have fun. "Shout out every crazy idea you can. Take other people's crazy ideas and add or tweak them." You'll be surprised how well it works. And if it doesn't, hey, you had some good laughs.

If you find your team is not open to this method, you might want to try another method called brainwriting. I first heard of brainwriting from Nina-Nike Velander, a communications expert on a webinar. The difference between brainstorming and brainwriting is quite brilliant. For one, it removes the intimidation factor. I tried this, and it also works well. This works basically the same as brainstorming, in that each person is generating ideas. Instead of saying your ideas aloud, you write them on a card (names not required). That card is passed to your team leader to comment without the concern of looking bad if that concerns you!

If you have a large group, I like to break them up into teams. Each team will review, and then explain their best idea(s) to the entire group. I love to have little prizes for the most unique idea, the funniest idea, and the top-voted idea. The key, however, is they all must be workable ideas, worth considering!

After you finish this brainstorming (or brainwriting) process, you should be able to identify and restate each other's best-case outcomes so that they are clear to each stakeholder involved in the evaluation or decision-making process. You're not going through this exercise to win an argument or promote disagreement or tear the solutions apart.

Instead, this process is about thinking through and developing even better potential solutions than the ones you and the others in your group initially proposed. These would have better outcomes and long-term WINX benefits. This is synergy at its best.

Take that Shower! Remember Dr. Ron Friedman's research. Let your subconscious mind work for you! Do this whenever you can, throughout each of the WINX steps.

Take Time to Think!

There are many ideas, stories, and methods in this book. Don't let me overwhelm you. The best advice I ever received was to learn everything I could, consider feedback, then put my own mind to work. So, don't forget the importance of taking time to think!

Some people have a special "think" place they go to, while some just write and write until the final answer appears. You may have your own way of stealing precious time to think. If you are working alone, or with a team, try to take at least a day for both focused thinking and activities (shower, workout, etc.) so your mind can do its magic.

What's next?

If you find a winner, great. Otherwise, pick your top two or three. You are ready for Step 5.

Step 5: Evaluate Alternatives

It's time to move from checkers to chess. At this point, you should have a handful of potential solutions. The best ones should rise to the top. They should be "no-brainers" but we are not ready to pick one just yet!

This step may be the shortest. However, it is THE solution component that makes you different, that earns loyalty, support, and long-term success.

Unfortunately, problems can be complex, and, if unresolved, they can snowball into multiple and aggressively more hurtful issues. So this step is critical to mitigating problems that are not addressed and triaged. This is why going deeper into this step involves thoroughly evaluating the potential impact on your customers, employees, and company.

In Step 3, you learned by understanding the complete situation (your current problem) and how that problem impacts all shareholders. You learned that before you take any action, it is important to evaluate the impact of that issue with a focus on:

- Your customers
- Your employees
- Your company

Then, in the problem-solving step, you went through a process or two to identify various solutions. It is now time to take your top three potential solutions and use the same method you used in Step 3. How will each of these potential solutions impact:

- Your customers
- Your employees
- Your company

You have either chosen your best solution or seen three or four possibilities. (The impact of a no-decision, and the impact of your two or three new alternative solutions.) Remember to use the free downloads at www.ParoneGroup.com/WINX. This WINX EVALUATING ALTERNATIVES FORM will be a game-changer. It is simple, yet allows you to see and assess the options you have worked so hard to identify against your problem statement, current situation, and BIG goal.

Now Tear the Solutions Apart

I know you thought you were done, and I promise you are very close.

Tearing your solutions apart can look like arguing against the decision. Here, identify the reverse impact. Play "Devil's Advocate." Try to shoot them down. Find the holes in the logic. Your goal is to make your recommendation "bulletproof." This may seem counterintuitive. But the better you are at finding the weakness in your decision and then correcting it, the better decision you will have created.

Prepare actions to deal best with the problems you identify. These action steps will help you prepare for any unintended outcomes in a later step. Each option has its pros and cons, even if you decide to stick with the current scenario (a no change). But staying ahead of any problems will allow you to be proactive rather than reactive.

Ideally, especially with massive decisions, this process will lead you to a WINX decision. For example, a decision that allows you to:

- Strongly support your customers,
- provide for the growth and revenue for your company,
- provide competitive (or hopefully better) wages and benefits from this culture of high value and service to all, and,
- is now a genuine WINX—that extends to everyone and their families!

Next, choose your top solution. Look at your problem statement, your BIG goal, and each option. You are ready to decide! Make your decision!

Now comes the big question:

Based on your decision, would you be able to survive if the worst possible outcomes you've imagined for the problem were to happen? This step helps you prepare for what you might face when implementing the solution and helps you ward off potentially worse problems. It may also help you make a better decision. First, take time to analyze your position, internally argue your position, and then share your position with others so they too can look for holes.

You've brainstormed ideas, solutions, and fixes for the problem and selected your top three to five solutions. This is when you begin to outline your plan of action and begin to tear the solutions apart, looking for what might not work, or the impact of each solution on each shareholder. What will you face when you announce the decision or implement the changes? What questions might you find yourself answering?

You are ready. Your work has paid off. You have identified the best solution of all options you identified.

Step 6: The Decision Step

"If you can't explain it simply, you don't understand it well enough"

— *Albert Einstein*

Organizations of all sizes will benefit from this book. So this section provides suggestions for those making decisions and, where appropriate, those supporting the decision-maker. For example, read on about a decision-maker who was frustrated with complaints vs. strategically thought through recommendations.

"I've instituted a new rule," Sam told me. "Don't come to me with a problem, complaint, or criticism unless you have a list of possible solutions, or at least an idea for a solution. I think it eliminates the whiners and malcontents," he said.

"How's that working out for you?" I asked.

"So far, so good," he said. "Complaints are down by 90 percent and people with legitimate complaints are providing some really interesting solutions. Things are getting done and morale is actually up."

Over time, Sam told me that people who initially hated the new policy began to embrace it, and even enjoy it. People who were tired of hearing co-workers complain all the time began to ask the complainer, "So, what's your solution?" Regardless of whether they cared about a solution or not, or they simply wanted the colleague to quit complaining didn't matter. The shift in thinking about problems did. Persistent complainers simply left when they realized no one wanted to hear them constantly complain, without offering solutions. All this resulted in a subtle change in the company culture—an unexpected benefit.

Taking responsibility and ownership for one's problems and environment empowers people and changes both work culture and personal and professional mindsets. While Sam's new rule may have seemed blunt and cruel to some employees, he accomplished exactly what he wanted—employee engagement and ownership in their jobs. When people had issues or problems, knowing they'd have to present a solution or potential solution to the problem caused them to actually think about the problem itself—often resulting in their answering or fixing the issue themselves. When Dwayne, a shipping clerk in the warehouse, began to complain about having to traverse across the warehouse for supplies several times each night, his co-workers reminded him of Sam's rule and for several hours Dwayne was silent.

After his break, he approached his supervisor and laid out the problem, including an estimate of the time he and other packers spent getting supplies. He suggested being allowed to use a forklift to move a pallet of boxes and packing items to the production line at the beginning of each shift.

He also went to his co-workers and ran his idea past them—discussing the "best" place to move the supplies too—so everyone benefited.

Two workers told Dwayne, "I hope this works. My back is killing me every night after carrying all those heavy bundles." Another worker mentioned how they'd have fewer boxes to recycle because the moisture and water that dripped on the boxes from being up against the warehouse wall would no longer be an issue.

As Dwayne shared all these comments with other co-workers, each one came up with other reasons to justify moving the supplies pallet.

By the time Dwayne spoke to Sam, reading the crew's reasons from the back of a paper lunch sack, he had a lengthy list of pros and cons.

Moving the supplies would reduce all the walking workers had to do. He pointed out that the strain on older workers' backs from carrying the boxes would be eliminated. This would result in fewer injuries. Not only was it safer, but having the supplies right at hand would save time. Sam agreed and let Dwayne move the pallet next to the line. It's now a permanent part of the shipping process.

While simply moving boxes and supplies doesn't seem like a big deal, the fact that Dwayne felt heard, and had his complaint and his idea recognized, empowered him and boosted his confidence. He began to look for other ways he could improve his workstation and help others. He liked hearing his co-workers tell him how much they appreciated not having to walk across the warehouse to carry boxes and supplies back and forth each night.

What Sam found out later was that somewhere along the line, the pallet of boxes and shipping supplies had been moved so machinery could be repaired and replaced and a new conveyor belt installed. That process had turned into an unexpected two-month-long process in which the packing supplies remained against the warehouse wall— out of the way of the engineers. Once the machinery was operational, no one thought to move the pallet of supplies back—and employees just continued to needlessly walk across the warehouse for supplies, until Dwayne brought it up.

Sam told me this story immediately when I explained WINX Step 6, "presenting the options to the decision-maker." What Dwayne had done in coming to him was to not only propose a solution—moving the packing supplies—but he also explained the pros and cons of his solution versus other options. He also explained various options he considered and why he recommended this particular solution. Like most of us do, he wanted to present enough evidence to justify and support his solution.

"I'd already figured out Dwayne's solution when he told me what his 'complaint' was," he said. "But I wanted to see what he'd say. I could have just said, 'Why not just move the supplies?' but he wouldn't have benefited from my giving him the answer. I was impressed that he not only came up with a solution, but with the pros and cons of the solution."

I use Sam and Dwayne's simple example of how to present a solution to a decision-maker because it clearly explains how and why presenting options to a decision-maker is needed:

- **It saves the decision-maker's time and resources.** Although Sam wouldn't have spent much time researching what needed to be done, not all problem/solution issues are so clearly defined. Leaders who try to do it all rarely progress.
- **It engages and involves those most likely to be impacted by the decision who know more about the pros and cons of the decision.** In this case, Dwayne and his crew were the ones most impacted by the solution, and by engaging them early in the process, Dwayne was able to get "buy-in" from them for his idea.
- **It opens up alternatives and solutions the decision-maker may not have considered.** Although the solution was pretty straightforward in this instance, not all problems are so easy to solve.

- **It leads to increased communication, empathy, and teamwork among employees.** By seeking out his crew's comments and talking to them, Dwayne inadvertently created a tighter bond with them by working on a solution that benefited them all.

- **It ensures that there are only viable, workable solutions being considered—cutting out the often creative, but unworkable solutions that come up during the research phase.** Dwayne and the crew had considered assigning one person, one of the younger, stronger crew members, to be the designated person to move boxes each shift. This would prevent having to shut down the line or have several members leave their stations to go get boxes.

- **If the problem has been accurately identified, it focuses the resources on eliminating the root cause and goals.** Dwayne's initial complaint was that he "had to walk five miles a night carrying heavy boxes." Some people, upon hearing this complaint, might assume Dwayne didn't like hard work or didn't want to do this part of his job. However, the root cause of the problem was not that workers had to carry heavy boxes across the warehouse—it was the fact the boxes weren't placed close enough to allow workers to do their jobs efficiently. The goal was to move the boxes closer to the shipping line to eliminate having to transport them by hand, not to eliminate them having to move the boxes at all. What was a subtle distinction in this instance can often balloon into larger, more expensive solutions when the goal is misidentified.

- **It shows whether the team understands the goal and the problem.** Dwayne and his crew understood the problem and the goal, but those supervisors assuming crews don't want to work, or who were complaining about the heavy boxes, may have misunderstood what the workers wanted. This could have resulted in the packing crews working on one goal—moving the boxes closer, and the supervisors looking for alternatives to eliminate anyone lifting boxes.

Journalist and author Chip Scanlon talks about how great journalists will "over-report"—and in a good way. In fact, he talks about over-reporting in his book: 33 *Ways Not to Screw Up Journalism*. As a reporter, he would research, investigate, and interview people—putting in a full day, week, or even month for what was often a short article. The work he put into finding and reporting a story was rarely reflected by the length of the story.

He suggested, "What most people never see is the over-reporting or the depth of research that goes into an article or story. They don't see the hard work, but they benefit from it. Without that background, those interviews, and that research, the story wouldn't be what it is. People see Olympic athletes win medals, but they don't see the years of sacrifice they put in to get to that medal. The Titanic wasn't sunk by the glacier above the water," he said. "It was sunk by the 80 percent of the ice that was under the water."

As thought-leaders and decision-makers, the same is true—it's the information, the consequences, and the facts we don't see at first glance that sink us. By looking at all the buried information, options, and concerns, we can avoid being blindsided by what we didn't see. When it's time for teams to report to and present the options and facts they found to the decision-maker, this is the process I've found works best—use the time to focus on how the recommendations, solutions, and alternatives you're presenting can make a difference for the organization, and don't worry about impressing senior management. It sounds obvious, but many teams seem to lose sight of the fact this is about the stakeholders, not advancing their own careers.

Construct your presentation with the audience—the decision-maker(s)—foremost in mind. Whether you are the decision-maker or the presenter, these tips hold true:

- Respect the decision-maker's time and keep as close to or a few minutes under the time allotted to make your presentation. If the presentation runs over schedule, it should come from the decision-maker's questions, not your lack of preparedness. Yes, the decision is important, but don't drag out the presentation or your alternatives for the sake of being in front of the decision-maker. Focus on the task at hand—the problem, the presentation, and the solutions. Identify and succinctly state the current problem, and explain what happens if we do nothing or the issue is not addressed. What will continue to happen (risk of status quo), or might likely happen if the problem is not addressed? Where possible, give time frames of potential impacts.
- List how the problem is currently being addressed, and what it's costing the company in terms of financial and capital resources, customer base, and employee impact. Explain what is and is not working and why it is or isn't if that is known.
- Start with the bottom line—costs: financial, capital, staffing, time, etc.
- Do your homework. Don't try to bluff your way through your presentation or the pros and cons of each alternative. You can't do this on the fly and make it up as you go along. If you need more time, ask for more time.
- If applicable, add a side-by-side comparison of the remaining status quo against the proposed change.

- State your reasons and thought process (why) for the solutions you're recommending.
- Timing matters. Where necessary and possible, point out to the decision-maker where problems can and will escalate rapidly if not dealt with quickly. Don't rush or push the decision-maker for a decision, but do include a timeframe for a decision as well. The old adage of "When you find yourself in a hole, stop digging," is true.
- Describe the anticipated impact of each proposed solution to all parties, including costs (risks of making the change), financial, branding, physical impacts, etc. You might include the WINX EVALUATING ALTERNATIVES FORM, found at www.ParoneGroup.com/WINX. If applicable, state what the other party or parties want or wanted.
- Be candid. If something won't work, or you think it's a weak alternative, say so. If you know something the decision-maker doesn't, or that the decision-maker appears not to understand like you think he should—say something. Don't hold back for fear of making him look ignorant, but don't treat him disrespectfully, either. The reason he tasked you (and your team) with finding alternatives and solutions is that he didn't have the time, skills, or resources to do so himself and because he trusts you to get the best information possible.
- Be prepared to be interrupted, to present facts, research, and data to back up your assertions or recommendations. Understand the decision-maker may spot, or think of, something different when listening to your presentation. Your ideas and research may even spark an alternative you didn't think of. That's not a loss—it's a collaboration. You may easily be asked to go back and explore additional alternatives or brainstorm new ideas that come up during the presentation. Good executives and decision-makers will demand the same from you as they would from themselves

when considering alternatives. Know what the decision-maker already knows, and more. Be ready to be questioned, even grilled, on your presentation, and don't fold. Memorize the numbers and have key facts written down on note cards so you don't forget, get confused, or leave something out. Where possible, use slides, greaseboards, or other systems to keep key points and data visible.

- Don't just present facts and data. Interpret what the facts and data mean in each particular situation or solution, so a relevant decision can be made. Don't use data and statistics to simply impress—make sure the statistics are included in the context of the issue. Tell the decision-makers what your numbers mean; don't assume they can interpret or plug the information into the solution. They're going to be looking for "the big picture and the bottom line." They depend on you to understand the data and interpret it for them. Some of the decision-makers will want to see the full analytics and research and some will not. No one wants to see you stop and "do the math" during your presentation unless it's to answer a question. However, if you prepared well enough, you should be able to anticipate those questions and already know the answers.

- Be flexible. You may be asked more questions about part of your presentation than you anticipated. If asked to dig deeper or pivot in an alternative direction, do so, regardless of what you may be thinking at the time. Most executives didn't get to where they are by being ill-prepared. Many of them may have a depth of understanding, experience, and expertise you know nothing about.

- Connect the dots, make the connections. Show the decision-maker you clearly understand the problem and each of your solutions. Tie your recommendations to the best alternatives —showing that you and your team support what the company values and that you're aligned with their decision-making criteria. State your alternatives clearly. Decision-makers don't want to guess what solutions go with which pros and cons. Separate and provide each alternative with the facts and details clearly stated.

After your presentation, the decision-maker may request more data, information, or research, or simply thank you and retreat to study your alternatives. It's unusual for a decision-maker to decide anything final during a presentation. Not making a decision is in itself a decision, but depending upon the decision to be made, taking time to weigh the alternatives is normal. Many executives will adopt a "wait and see" attitude before making a decision. This is precisely why it is important to share the impact of the current situation (no change) against the proposed solutions. Use subtle reminders that no decision is, in fact, a decision that might be causing harm. If a decision(s) is unnecessarily delayed or postponed, a number of options and alternatives may be eliminated or changed significantly, and control over the situation will be lost. You may lose the opportunity to hire a specific candidate, miss a filing date, or miss out on a new technology trend. If time is important in any aspect of your findings, end your presentation with that information. Then, put a date and time on each alternative, as in: "To implement this decision you'd need to decide on it and begin implementing it by such and such a date." Include this "expiration date" in all written documentation as well.

Whether you have successfully presented alternatives to the decision-maker, or you are the decision-maker reviewing a presentation of options, it's important the focus remains on the problem, the solution, and the decision, not on influencing executives to satisfy an agenda, curry favor, or impress leadership by focusing more on what they want rather than on what the executive needs. It may be brutal to raise that issue, but I've seen it happen enough to make it a point to address it.

A note for the decision-maker: Remember that your team worked hard and long on this project. Show your appreciation and encouragement. Otherwise, you may not get the same enthusiasm on your next problem-solving journey.

The Decision Maker - Making the Final Decision

Your team has put a lot of time and effort into this process. They made their decision and have proposed a WINX recommendation. All of the work that has gone into this process should be outlined and clear, but the buck stops with you. Ask questions if you have them. Think through the consequences of your decisions. Hospitals that once fired nurses for not getting the COVID vaccine are now allowing other employees with COVID to tend to patients because of a health care shortage.[1]

The decision-maker has the responsibility to ensure they check the boxes. Know what those boxes are for you. There are no guarantees in life, but at this point, they want to feel confident that the problem-solving process worked as intended. Some decisions, most, in fact, are better made by those who must live with the decision. For example, when hiring, you want Human Resources to ensure legal and policy boxes are checked, then the manager actually responsible for the new employee makes the final decision based on those that pass the HR review. You could weigh in, but is it in your best interest and in the best use of your time to do so? Delegate decisions to those best equipped to make them, and for whom you trust to take responsibility for the results. Remember, however, to be sure they understand the WINX strategy and focus on all parties. The customer, employees, and company.

Don't Make Decisions Out of Fear or Pressure

As we saw with NASA and Morton Thiokol and the space shuttle *Challenger* decision, and with Ford Motors and the Pinto decision, bad decisions are made when there is personal, economic, and political pressure to make an expedient decision, not the right or ethical decision. Don't buckle to pressure of any kind—real or perceived. Why is there always enough time to "do it over" if there's never enough time to "do it right"? Force yourself to slow down and really look at your decision, your issue, and the possible outcomes. I promise you'll make better, wiser decisions when you do.

If I can urge you to do one thing to expand your awareness about this part of the decision-making process, it's to go back and learn about the decision-making process and lessons around the *Challenger* disaster, beginning with this *Forbes* article on the "lasting leadership lessons learned."[2]

Yielding to pressure rarely works. A primary contractor reversed its opinion and recommended the shuttle launch, contrary to the strenuous safety concerns of at least four of its engineers. That was done to accommodate a major customer of the contractor. Effective risk evaluation processes typically involve "give and take" exchanges with various interested parties, but provide protection against the excessive influence of purely financial pressures.[3]

Weigh the Cost of Failure

Failure is a part of life. We all experience it and hopefully learn from it and move on, doing better "the next time." And there will be a next time! By honestly weighing and preparing for consequences, you can, believe it or not, soften the blow of failure a bit. If failing was/is a possibility, it won't come as such a shock, and you may be better prepared to step back and have another run at a better solution.

Society was built on failure. Weighing the cost of failure doesn't mean you're wrong, weak, or unable to make good decisions. It means you're learning and improving.

In 1960, before George Steinbrenner won entry into six World Series between 1996 and 2003 and boasted a record as one of the most profitable teams in Major League Baseball, he owned a minor basketball team called the Cleveland Pipers. By 1962 he had bankrupted an entire franchise. He led a losing streak for twenty years before finally becoming known as the coach of the winningest team in baseball—The New York Yankees.[4]

Steve Jobs had astounding success in his twenties, yet was fired from his own company by his board of directors, before bouncing back again with a new company, NeXT, which Apple acquired, along with Jobs. What looked like total failure was just a step along the path.

I could name dozens of people and companies who failed and rose again from the ashes to succeed beyond anyone's wildest dreams. What matters is not that you fail, but that you don't let failure stop you. You get up and keep going.

Failure is just a chance to learn and grow. When you first start implementing the WINX system, you may be surprised to realize you've had a string of successes, followed by failures as you learn how to pinpoint challenges and issues, and dig to find the "real" challenge and not just what appears to be the issue. The more often you follow the steps, the better you'll get. You'll learn from your failures and eventually learn to recognize the gift that failure can be. It makes you more aware, more conscious, and more motivated to tackle the next decision—I guarantee it.

Blend Head-Smart and Gut-Smart Decisions

It's important to collect, examine, and tear your solutions apart in search of the best alternative based on research. You'll make better decisions by turning to facts, weighing the pros and cons, and getting input from others. There will be times you'll need to rely to some degree on your "gut" feelings or intuition as well as cold, hard facts. From this collaborative vantage point, you will find healthier, sustainable decisions.

In speaking about intuition, years ago I was with a client named Jeff, and he shared the story of a firefighting captain who began to cross the roof of a house to cut open a hole for other firefighters to get their hoses into the home. The moment he stepped off the ladder, onto the roof, and took two steps, he began yelling for everyone to leave the house and get away from the scene. His voice was commanding and urgent. No fire had breached the roof, and to all outside accounts, he and his men were doing everything "by the book" in terms of attacking and fighting the fire.

However, minutes after he gave the command and was on the ground running away, the entire house collapsed on itself. Had he and his men been on the roof or inside, they would have all perished or been severely burned.

In the aftermath of the collapse, he couldn't tell his chief why he gave the order. "Something just didn't feel right," he said. After much reflection, the chief learned the captain had been on several house fires where roofs collapsed. His body remembered the structures' feeling, sensation, and "feel" just before their collapse. That feeling didn't come out of thin air. It was intuition. And intuition is simply our subconscious reminding us of what we have already experienced and are about to experience again.

Author and researcher Jeremy Sherman explains in an article for *Psychology Today*, "Intuition is a process that gives us the ability to know something directly without analytic reasoning, bridging the gap between the conscious and nonconscious parts of our mind, and also between instinct and reason."[5]

As you begin to make more conscious decisions, you'll find yourself using both your head and heart (intuition) to make decisions. Depending on your personality, you may learn more about a left-brain (logical) decision-making style versus an intuitive (creative/intuitive) style. What works is what works for you and your team. Don't be afraid to be open to both styles when making a decision. There will be times when you don't have time to collect facts or weigh the pros and cons. On 9/11, people mostly followed their instincts. Many ignored them. Where at all possible, use facts and the WINX process, but never be afraid to consider "hunches" or intuition when you get ready to act.

Step 7: Prepare For Impact

"If you prepare yourself at every point as well as you can...you will be able to grasp opportunity for broader experience when it appears."

— Eleanor Roosevelt

My plane was taxiing out to the airfield where we'd launch into the air shortly after the flight attendant's safety talk. As the attendant was explaining how to put on your seatbelt and to wear it for turbulence, as well as how to "prepare for impact," the gentleman sitting next to me yawned. He said, "I don't know why they even bother to tell us that, because no one survives a crash." I reminded him of the passengers on Captain Chesley Sullenberger's flight ten years ago.

In an amazing feat of flying skill, Captain "Sully" landed his plane on the Hudson River with no fatalities and only minor injuries. They, I told the gentleman, might disagree with his assessment. The emergency landing of the plane after striking a flock of birds left all

150 passengers and 5 crew members alive and well and no worse for the impact.[1]

"Yeah, maybe," he said. "But in a real impact, no one is going to survive. Telling us to prepare for impact just gives us something to do. It gives people false hope so they don't run up and down the aisle trying to get out of the plane. All that 'grab your ankles and duck your head' stuff does is make it easier for them to recover our bodies after the crash."

I didn't know how to respond, but we agreed to disagree and moved on to other things. However, his response to "prepare for impact" made me curious, so later, back in my hotel room, I Googled it. Does preparing for impact make a difference? What I found was, "it depends." It depends on the situation, the placement of the passengers, the age, weight, size of the passenger, and a lot of variables that I'm not going to go into here.

What mattered to me was that I learned that whether a person was in a vehicle of any kind, from a carnival ride to public transportation, the best anyone could do was prepare for impact, but more importantly, to have a plan to deal with the event and aftermath *after* the impact. In other words, if you're going to hit something, there's not a whole lot you can do to guarantee things are going to go well.

Airline flight attendants are taught how to prepare for the physical impact, but more importantly, knowing what to do after that impact.

You can prepare your employees, customers, and company for the impact of your decisions, but it's just as critical to prepare equally well for what happens after the impact—or decision.

In the process of learning about how airlines "prepare passengers for impact," I also learned there are now airlines where planes have airbags for passengers in the event of a crash or impact. And, new laws require that passenger seats are able to withstand sixteen times more force than before—so they aren't torn out on impact.

The takeaway for me was, to do all you can to prepare for impact but keep improving your preparations for surviving the impact, and then have a plan in place to deal with the fallout.

Since you have completed Steps 1 through 6, now it's time to "prepare for impact." Whatever your role, relax. You know you've given it your full focus and settled on the best options. Does that mean the hard work is over? No.

"Prepare for impact" means just that—prepare for the impact. You know that the *positive* of your decision outweighed the negative, yet very, very few decisions run 100 percent smoothly. The more people who are impacted by your decisions, the greater the likelihood there will be pushback. Be ready for it and you can reduce the fallout.

Complaints, lost clients, or employees, whatever it is, look it in the face and be prepared. Should you advise in advance? How? When? The reason some companies get **stuck** with things as they are, afraid to make changes, is that there can be negative as well as positive consequences, and they fear the worst. Better to "live with the devil you know, than the devil you don't know," as the saying goes.

For CVS, their challenge was not only preparing their employees for the public's reaction to their decision to pull all tobacco from their stores, but they also needed to prepare for the reaction to that announcement (impact), and then prepare for the aftermath—media and customer reactions, angry smokers, happy customers who welcomed the change, and every possible scenario corporate could imagine.

Face the impact before it hits. In other words, *get ahead of it*, and make sure you are all on the same page, providing the same message. The more challenging the decision, the more preparation is needed for your entire team. Remember, you spent hours, possibly months, or more evaluating options and data for this project. The rest of your team may be hearing of the decision for the first time. Help them understand the why. Your team will have more impact on the success or failure of your decision than some can imagine. Especially if they are customer-facing.

> "A clear vision must be developed in order to inspire, motivate, and activate people to move the business forward together."

> — Roland Wijnen

Step 8: Implement The Decision

"The way to get started is to quit talking and begin doing."

— Walt Disney

"You have a decision to make," I told Sarah, an HR director for a small company expanding its workforce.

She rolled her eyes and sighed heavily. "I know," she said. "And I'm unsure how to make it. I can see the pros and cons of both sides, and one decision looks as good as the other. How do I choose?"

"Just pick one," I said. "Go with your gut. If you can't logically defend either decision, just trust your intuition and decide. You have all the information you need to make a decision, and at this point, any additional information isn't going to move the bar enough to matter. Also, remember that *not* choosing is also a decision."

Believe it or not, that conversation happens more than you'd think, especially among compassionate, caring executives, both male and female, who truly want to make the "best decision."

The difference between a "good" and an "okay" decision can sometimes be small, and chances are either one truly would be a good decision. These include hiring decisions. Hiring the right person or people should be a critical decision, along with decisions about opportunities. But those small decisions can have huge impacts down the road. Don't imagine a "simple" decision is ever really simple. Do your due diligence, gather and evaluate, find alternative solutions, tear those solutions apart, and make your decision based on what you know and the information you have at the time you're making it. I quoted my friend Becky, a senior organizational effectiveness consultant for a major hospital, who said to me when looking at titles for this book, "Sometimes you just need to put a period on it!"

"Whew! We're done," Sarah told me a week later. "We're done interviewing candidates and have made our decision. We've selected five new hires, and all we have left to do is *implement the decision* like you said—hire them and launch the project." She sighed happily.

"Congratulations!" I said. "Implementation can be the most stressful but exciting part of any decision-making. You've put in the hard work, and now you're about to reap the benefits of your investment. So what comes next?"

The onboarding process, employee reviews, and other actions are already in place for most companies and automatically kick in with the hiring. However, not all hires go smoothly. Other decisions must be made down the road as each new employee comes on—some for promotions, others requiring training, and so on.

Remember, the decision-making process doesn't end once the decision is made, any more than a chess game is over once that first chess piece is moved. The "game" is ongoing, with more decisions to be made at each stage. Every decision creates new ripples that eventually require additional decisions. That's how life and business work and why learning to make and implement smart decisions is critical.

The WINX process is focused on making decisions, and one of the most critical steps is the final step—implementing your decisions.

Implementation usually involves date setting, scheduling, and a structured plan that requires more decisions—who will be in charge of implementing a decision? When will the decision be implemented? How will we know if we made the right decision—and in a timely enough fashion to pivot and change or adjust things to avoid a bad decision?

Those questions, and others, are why an implementation plan not only ensures you also keep yourself on track, but allows you to see your progress or lack of movement around your decision.

Implementation Planning

There are many benefits to implementation planning—the top one being an increased chance of project success. Implementation plans prevent new issues from occurring or help resolve them quickly when they do come up.

When you have a plan, communication and team focus are better, resources are used more wisely, things flow better, goals are reached more easily, and accountability is better since everyone knows who is responsible for what. I can't overstress the importance of implementing your decision well. No matter how great the decision you've made is, it's worthless if you can't implement it well.

Implementation is more than just an action you take, a memo you issue, or a command you give. Implementation is a detailed plan, often referred to as your "strategic plan." This plan should outline the steps needed to accomplish or launch your decision. This plan combines strategy, process, and action and will include all project parts, from scope to budget and beyond. Implemented decisions require planning, action, and follow-up to be successful:

• Define your goals or the objective of the decision.

• Assign implementation manager(s), and necessary roles to team members.

• Schedule milestones:

○ Assign responsibilities and tasks to each team member.

○ Track responsibilities in a shared document, possibly using either a Gantt Chart or spreadsheet to track your progress.

• Conduct routinely scheduled meetings to stay on top of accountability and questions. Learning after the fact a task or project has not been completed on time or as expected can set you up for failure.

• And before you put a period on this project, schedule a shake-out date. This is a time that is on your calendar, for example, sixty days after implementation to assess any tweaks or adjustments that should be made.

Depending on the complexity and scope of your decision, implementing and managing that decision can be difficult, time-consuming, and often confusing. If you're not sure how to create an implementation plan for your particular decisions and projects, there are many project management tools online that can walk you through the process. Any project management software that helps you plan, organize, and manage your team's work, from start to finish, and acts as a collaboration point will work. The software should:

- Be accessible to all team members in real-time.
- Streamline communication among team members.
- Coordinate team tasks, so everyone knows who's doing what.
- Improve collaboration by allowing everyone to share feedback, files, and status updates.

- Give team members a complete view of what needs to be done, so tasks are accomplished in order and on time.
- Help keep everyone on track and
- Have export functions that allow you to compile data on your progress for a post-decision report.

The Winx Post-Decision Review – Shaking it out!

Remember, decisions don't control or monitor themselves. Whether you decide to implement a new branding strategy, hire or fire new vendors, or launch a new research and development project, someone has to ensure that the decision is not only made, but implemented, managed, evaluated, reported on, and followed up on so future decisions can be made based on the success or failure of that WINX process.

Don't hesitate to conduct a "Post Decision Report" for large or small decisions. This post-decision review might include:

- a summary of the challenge/problem statement,
- the goal intended,
- consequences and outcome of the decision,
- anything that went well or didn't go well,
- any tweaks needed, and action to be taken.

This review can be as simple or elaborate as you and your culture/personnel decide. Do what works for you.

Most post-decision reviews can be covered and documented on one page for simple decisions or up to several or more pages for more complex challenges. Significant decisions may involve lengthy, complex reports.

Either way, the report itself should be simple and brief.

I've included a sample of a simple POST DECISION REVIEW report that can be found at www.ParoneGroup.com/WINX if you want to use that template or create your own as it works best for you.

Some may choose to add additional information to help with lessons learned and developmental training. If so, you can document the effectiveness/ineffectiveness of the decision by asking and answering the following questions:

1. Did it work? Did you meet or exceed your goals at the time the decision was made? Are there other things to consider, over and beyond the WINX process? Possibly circumstances have changed.
2. Were there any problems, what were they, and how were they handled?
3. Did you fail to consider something important?
4. What would you change the next time?
5. What did you learn?
6. What did you wish you'd known, asked, questioned, or investigated before/during this process?
7. Who were the team members involved, and what role did they play? Who were the most influential members, and why?

Based on the circumstances, remind yourself and your team of the end goal, the progress, the wins, and the losses along the way. Otherwise, it's easy to lose focus. This is not a time to assign blame or focus on failures or oversights. It's time to learn how to correct the process and determine what better actions you will implement the next time.

So, while you may feel a great sense of relief at reaching the eighth step of the WINX process, the process continues—"rinse and repeat," as the saying goes.

At least once a quarter, take time to review the WINX process and how successful, or not, it has been. Some companies do this more frequently, depending on how many significant decisions they need to make. New companies and start-ups may meet weekly, and larger, more established companies may meet once a quarter. Again, there are no hard or fast rules other than what works with your company and culture.

Mastering WINX is an iterative process—where most companies learn in increments or stages. Make this a fun time, a time of sharing stories, lessons learned, failures as well as successes. While you may think this is overkill, remember that lessons learned can reduce a lot of pain in the future. Circulate, where appropriate, a company newsletter or at least a supervisor review with a brief post-decision report and follow-up.

As much as possible, engage your employees, your executives, and your staff with the process. Having employees who understand the process and are engaged with the WINX steps will result in better employees and better outcomes. Some employees may find it helpful to apply the WINX process to their home/family life. Simply replace the stakeholders. As one example in place of customers, employees, and company, yours may be husband, wife, children.

Decision-making is a skill, and like any skill, it must be practiced to become effective. I assure you, it gets easier every time you go through the eight steps. By sharing our efforts, insights, and experiences (good, bad, or indifferent), we all benefit and get better with each new decision we make, each new challenge we face, and each new failure that seems to dog our heels.

Start with small decisions to get the feel of the process. Don't neglect a post-decision report—even if it's just a "one-pager" with a few sentences about each step. And most of all, if you find this book and the process has helped you and your company, family, or business (large or small), please take time to share the book with someone and let colleagues know it had an impact on you.

We all learn by teaching, so remember to take time and train others on your team, or ask us to do that for you. Some larger companies have formed small groups to share the steps with co-workers. Decisions don't have to be big, nor do high-ranking employees need to come up with ideas that can impact that change in the lives of many.

One team, on the same train moving in the same direction, is a powerful force!

Forms and Images

THE FOCUSED TRIO

Downloadable and reusable forms can be found at:
www.ParoneGroup.com/WINX. We will include additional
resources as they become available.

A self-assessment can be found at:
www.ParoneGroup.com/WINXAssessment

The following are images of the forms for a quick reference.

WINX Problem Solving Model Checklist

Use this form starting with STEP 1 to keep you on track throughout the problem-solving model as you work on problems or projects.

COMPANY	Click or tap here to enter text.
Problem Statement	Click or tap here to enter text.
Big Goal in Resolving the Problem	Click or tap here to enter text.

Start date	Click or tap to enter a date.	Closed	Click or tap to enter a date.
Project Leader	Click or tap here to enter text.		

☐	1	**Craft Your Problem Statement** (My problem statement has clear and easily understood by others without asking for clarification)
☐	2	**Examine the Root Cause** (The problem statement addresses the root cause)
☐	3	**Evaluate the Impact of the Current Problem** ☐ We have evaluated the impact of the current problem and found that the issue needs NO further action. (or) ☐ we have determined that the this issue requires further action
☐	4	**Problem Solving** (We have completed the problem-solving processes and listed up to 3 alternatives, evaluating the impact on all stakeholders)
☐	5	**Evaluate Alternatives** (We have evaluated the alternatives against the current problem and documented our recommendation(s) based on our big goal and the best long-term solution.)
☐	6	**The Decision Step** ☐ We have prepared our recommendation(s) and are ready to present ☐ The decision is approved (continue to step(s) below) or ☐ More work is required (start with step 1)
☐	7	**Prepare for Impact** We have Prepared for Impact
☐	8	**Implement the Decision** ☐ Goals documented ☐ Assignments made ☐ Timelines established ☐ Tracking document established ☐ A date is on the calendar for the POST-DECISION review ☐ Issue is CLOSED ☐ Post-Decision review completed.

WINX Problem Solving Idea Generator

Use this form starting with STEP 1 to keep you on track throughout the problem-solving model as you work on problems or projects.

COMPANY	Click or tap here to enter text.
Problem Statement	Click or tap here to enter text.

☐	1	**Redefine What it Means to Win:** Click or tap here to enter text.
☐	2	**Are You In Danger of a Single Story?** Click or tap here to enter text.
☐	3	**Can You Simply Pivot?** Click or tap here to enter text.
☐	4	**What Stakeholders can Provide Feedback or Ideas?** Click or tap here to enter text.
☐	5	**Can You Consult with People Who Think Differently?** Click or tap here to enter text.
☐	6	**Are You Holding Yourself Back (Face Uncertainty)** Click or tap here to enter text.
☐	7	**Brainstorming Session** Click or tap here to enter text.
☐	8	**Brainwriting Session** Click or tap here to enter text.
☐	9	**Employee Surveys** Click or tap here to enter text.
☐	10	**Customer Surveys** Click or tap here to enter text.
☐	11	**Take a Break (showers, walk, other non-focused activities)** Click or tap here to enter text.

		Include Your Ideas or Resources Below **Human Resources, Available Consultant, Expert in Field, Religious Support, etc.**
☐	1	Click or tap here to enter text.
☐	2	Click or tap here to enter text.
☐	3	Click or tap here to enter text.
☐	4	Click or tap here to enter text.

WINX Evaluating Alternatives Form

Use this form for STEP 5 to evaluate the impact of your current problem or situation against possible solutions and make your decision. (yellow fields indicate they can be edited)

COMPANY	Click or tap here to enter text.
Start Date	Click or tap to enter a date.

Project Leader Click or tap here to enter text.	Impact on Customers	Impact on Employees	Impact on Company	Notes	
Problem Statement Click or tap here to enter text.	**Pro** Click or tap here to enter text. **Con** Click or tap here to enter text.	**Pro** Click or tap here to enter text. **Con** Click or tap here to enter text.	**Pro** Click or tap here to enter text. **Con** Click or tap here to enter text.	Click or tap here to enter text.	**WINX BIG Goal** Click or tap here to enter text.
Solution Option 1 Click or tap here to enter text.	**Pro** Click or tap here to enter text. **Con** Click or tap here to enter text.	**Pro** Click or tap here to enter text. **Con** Click or tap here to enter text.	**Pro** Click or tap here to enter text. **Con** Click or tap here to enter text.	Click or tap here to enter text.	
Solution Option 2 Click or tap here to enter text.	**Pro** Click or tap here to enter text. **Con** Click or tap here to enter text.	**Pro** Click or tap here to enter text. **Con** Click or tap here to enter text.	**Pro** Click or tap here to enter text. **Con** Click or tap here to enter text.	Click or tap here to enter text.	**Decision** Click or tap here to enter text.
Solution Option 3 Click or tap here to enter text.	**Pro** Click or tap here to enter text. **Con** Click or tap here to enter text.	**Pro** Click or tap here to enter text. **Con** Click or tap here to enter text.	**Pro** Click or tap here to enter text. **Con** Click or tap here to enter text.	Click or tap here to enter text.	

WINX POST-DECISION Review

Use this form to plan & record your follow-up on the post-decision process in STEP 8. You can also record success, lessons learned, and other information to help you in future reviews or like-type decisions.

COMPANY	Click or tap here to enter text
Initial Problem Statement	Click or tap here to enter text.
Initial WINX Goal in Resolving the Problem	Click or tap here to enter text.

| Date of Last Review | Click or tap to enter a date. |
| Project Leader | Click or tap here to enter text. |

□ 1 **Which option did you choose:**
Click or tap here to enter text.

□ 2 **Were your results successful:**
Click or tap here to enter text.

□ 3 **Pros of decision:**
Click or tap here to enter text.

□ 4 **Lessons learned that you would do differently next time:**
Click or tap here to enter text.

□ 5 **List any tweaks or changes needed:**
Click or tap here to enter text.

□ 6 **If tweaks or follow up are needed, have you assigned responsibility or scheduled follow-up?:**
Click or tap here to enter text.

□ 7 **Additional Notes (lessons learned, what you wish you had known, asked, questioned, or investigated before or during this process – most influential team members etc.)**
Click or tap here to enter text.

□ 8 **Next date of review (or indicate if resolved):**
Click or tap here to enter text.

Before You Go

"Real happiness comes from sharing what you've learned with people who matter."

— *Unknown*

It has been an honor and a pleasure sharing my experiences as a busy executive and as someone who was once upon a time a working mother and a new employee. We all start at the beginning.

The world needs you and the significant impact you have to make. My goal is to help you and others find the motivation and opportunities to win in big ways. Exponential wins that extend to customers, employees, our company and shareholders, our vendors, and ultimately our families and communities. The opportunities are endless and all start with you! I hope the time you spent reading this book energizes you and propels you forward.

Please reach out to me with any questions you might have through LinkedIn or preferably through my website at: www.ParoneGroup.com/contact.

I'm also available for speaking engagements and consulting. I look forward to hearing from you.

Finally, If you found this book helpful, please consider going to Amazon and leaving a review. Even a short paragraph or your favorite takeaways might be helpful for those that would like new ideas. I would be most grateful!

At your service,

About The Author

Irma Parone is a sought-after leadership consultant, certified speaker, and international best-selling author. A graduate of Cornell University's Industrial Relations Studies Program, and Institute of Organizational Development OD Certified Professional, she is the CEO of Parone Group. Parone is also heavily involved in volunteering in her community. For the Coral Springs, Coconut Creek Regional Chamber of Commerce, Parone serves on the Board of Trustees, Ambassador & Education Committees, & VP of Education for their Toastmasters Group. Additional volunteer services include serving on the Career Placement Services Advisory Committee for Atlantic Technical College, Interview Volunteer for Students with the Virtual Enterprises International, Inc, and a volunteer for Kindness Shared Happiness Squared.

She has successfully helped companies improve company culture, increase customer retention, and reduce employee turnover for well over two decades

Her insights have been included in a chapter in the international bestseller *"Voices of the 21st Century: Bold, Brave, and Brilliant Women Who Make a Difference."*

Acknowledgments

This book would have not been possible without the support, guidance, care, and influence of the following individuals. I cannot thank them enough for the roles they played in my life.

First, thank you to my parents, Jerry and Alda Parone, who grounded and loved me. I miss you every day!

Thanks to my career influencers Jack Collins and Leonard Kline. The many years of learning from you were invaluable in my development.

Thank you for your special support and motivation throughout this book journey: Professor Suzanne Lambert, Author and Coach Jan (Sunny) Simon, and Author and Talent Strategist Dr. Desiree Aragon.

To multiple best-selling author and international speaker Akash Karia. Thank you for teaching me so much about writing and speaking, and convincing me to do this. And for your generosity of time. You are appreciated!

Acknowledgments

Thank you, Women Speakers Association, for helping me become an international bestselling author, as a Co-Author in *Voices of the 21st Century: Bold, Brave, and Brilliant Women Who Make a Difference.*

Thank you, Robert Catalano and the Spearhead Group Design team for creating my WINX triangular view design.

And thank you Melissa G Wilson, for taking me through my final book-creation process, utilizing your many expert resources in writing and publishing hundreds of books.

Finally, thanks to my son, Durski (Carl J. Fidurski, 11), who inspired my book cover and always gave me great ideas. I love you!

Notes

Introduction

1. Morse, Gardiner. "Decisions and Desire." Harvard Business Review. Accessed April 14, 2022. https://hbr.org/2006/01/decisions-and-desire
2. Ibid
3. Ibid
4. Ibid

Good, Bad, Ugly, or Awesome; We Are the Decisions We Make

1. CEO Today Magazine website. "8 of the Worst Business Decisions Ever Made." CEO Today. Accessed April 14, 2022. https://www.ceotodaymagazine.com/2018/08/8-of-the-worst-business-decisions-ever-made/
2. Hoffman, Claire. "Blockbuster.com Is Sued By Netflix." Los Angeles Times. Accessed April 14, 2022. https://www.latimes.com/archives/la-xpm-2006-apr-05-fi-netflix5-story.html
3. Hast, Tim. "Kill Your Business in Five Easy Steps; Be a Blockbuster." Encore Life Skills. June 22, 2018. http://encorelifeskills.com/kill-your-business-in-five-easy-steps-be-a-blockbuster/
4. IMDB Website. "E.T. The Extra-Terrestrial: Trivia." IMDB. Accessed April 14, 2022. https://www.imdb.com/title/tt0083866/trivia/
5. Ibid
6. Ibid
7. Ibid
8. Ibid
9. Haden, Jeff. "J.K. Rowling Says 1 Decision Separates People Who Achieve Success From Those Who Only Dream." Inc.com. Accessed April 14, 2022. https://www.inc.com/jeff-haden/jk-rowling-says-1-decision-separates-people-who-achieve-success-from-those-who-only-dream.html
10. Johnson, Simon. "J.K. Rowling regrets her mother never knew Harry Potter." The Telegraph. Accessed April 14, 2022. https://www.telegraph.co.uk/news/celebritynews/2445281/JK-Rowling-regrets-her-mother-never-knew-Harry-Potter.html
11. CEO Today Magazine website. "8 of the Worst Business Decisions Ever Made." CEO Today. Accessed April 14, 2022. https://www.ceotodaymagazine.com/2018/08/8-of-the-worst-business-decisions-ever-made/
12. Dallas News Administrator. "Lost legacy: 50 years after its founding, EDS name has evaporated." Dallasnews.com. Accessed April 14, 2022. https://www.

dallasnews.com/business/2012/12/09/lost-legacy-50-years-after-its-founding-eds-name-has-evaporated/

13. CEO Today Magazine website. "8 of the Worst Business Decisions Ever Made." CEO Today. Accessed April 14, 2022. https://www.ceotodaymagazine.com/2018/08/8-of-the-worst-business-decisions-ever-made/ https://www.ceotodaymagazine.com/2018/08/8-of-the-worst-business-decisions-ever-made/

14. Powerball.com Website. "Winner Stories." Powerball.com. Accessed April 14, 2022. https://www.powerball.com/winner-stories

15. Marte, Jonnelle. "How not to squander the $1.5 billion Powerball jackpot." Washington Post. Accessed April 14, 2022. https://www.washingtonpost.com/news/get-there/wp/2016/01/08/how-not-to-squander-the-800-million-powerball-jackpot/

16. Imbens, Guido W., Ruben, Donald B. and Sacerdotem Bruce I. "Estimating the Effect of Unearned Income on Labor Earnings, Savings and Consumption: Evidence From a Survey of Lottery Players." American Economic Association. Accessed April 14, 2022. https://www.aeaweb.org/articles?id=10.1257/aer.91.4.778

17. Hess, Abigail Johnson. "Here's why lottery winners go broke." CNBC.com August 25, 2017. https://www.cnbc.com/2017/08/25/heres-why-lottery-winners-go-broke.html

18. Godin, Seth. "Unreasonable Clients." Seth's Blog. Accessed April 14, 2022. https://seths.blog/2013/09/unreasonable-clients/

19. Ibid

20. Ibid

21. Russell, Connair and Muthukrishna, Michael. "The Secret To Innovation Is Our Collective Brain." Evonomics.com. Accessed April 14, 2022. https://evonomics.com/secret-to-innovation-is-our-collective-brain/

22. Gordon, John Steele. "How the Industrial Revolution Began." Barrons.com. Accessed April 14, 2022. https://www.barrons.com/articles/SB51367578116875004693704580451923366491204

23. Poetz, Marion, Franke, Nicolaus and Schreier, Martin. "Sometimes the Best Ideas Come From Outside Your Industry." Harvard Business Review. Accessed April 14, 2022. https://hbr.org/2014/11/sometimes-the-best-ideas-come-from-outside-your-industry

24. Vedantam, Shankar, Schmidt, Jennifer, Shah, Parth and Boyle, Tara. "Creativity And Diversity: How Exposure To Different People Affects Our Thinking." NPR.org. July 27, 2020. https://www.npr.org/2020/07/27/895858974/creativity-and-diversity-how-exposure-to-different-people-affects-our-thinking

25. Poetz, Marion, Franke, Nicolaus and Schreier, Martin. "Sometimes the Best Ideas Come From Outside Your Industry." Harvard Business Review. Accessed April 14, 2022. https://hbr.org/2014/11/sometimes-the-best-ideas-come-from-outside-your-industry

26. Ibid

27. Philosophia.ucng.edu Website. "Case: The Ford Pinto." Philosophia.ucng.edu. Accessed April 14, 2022. https://philosophia.uncg.edu/phi361-matteson/module-1-why-does-business-need-ethics/case-the-ford-pinto/

28. Reiff Law Firm Website. "Ford's Fiery Pintos Lead to Injuries, Deaths and Lawsuits." reifflawfirm.com. Accessed April 14, 2022. https://www.reifflawfirm.

com/fords-fiery-pintos-lead-injuries-deaths-lawsuits/

29. Orangebean Indiana Website. "Three Girls Gone: the Ford Pinto and Indiana v. Ford Motor Company. Oranbebeanindiana.com. September 4, 2019. https://orangebeanindiana.com/2019/09/04/three-girls-gone-the-pinto-and-indiana-v-ford-motor-co/

30. Ibid.

31. Ibid

32. Reiff Law Firm Website. "Ford's Fiery Pintos Lead to Injuries, Deaths and Lawsuits." reifflawfirm.com. Accessed April 14, 2022. https://www.reifflawfirm.com/fords-fiery-pintos-lead-injuries-deaths-lawsuits/

33. Orangebean Indiana Website. "Three Girls Gone: the Ford Pinto and Indiana v. Ford Motor Company. Oranbebeanindiana.com. September 4, 2019. https://orangebeanindiana.com/2019/09/04/three-girls-gone-the-pinto-and-indiana-v-ford-motor-co/

34. Teitel, Amy Shira. "What Caused the Challenger Disaster?" History.com. January 28, 2022. https://www.history.com/news/how-the-challenger-disaster-changed-nasa

35. Berkes, Howard. "Remembering Allan McDonald: He Refused to Approve Challenger Launch, Exposed Cover-up." NPR.com. March 7, 2021. https://www.npr.org/2021/03/07/974534021/remembering-allan-mcdonald-he-refused-to-approve-challenger-launch-exposed-cover

36. Ibid

37. Ibid

38. Hobson, Karolina. "Five Reasons Employees Are Your Company's No. 1 Asset." Forbes.com. December 12, 2019. https://www.forbes.com/sites/forbesbusinessdevelopmentcouncil/2019/12/12/five-reasons-employees-are-your-companys-no-1-asset/

Overview Of The Winx Process: An 8-Step Framework to Decision Making

1. PR Newswire Website. "New DDI Research: 57 Percent of Employees Quit Because of Their Boss." PRNewswire.com. Accessed April 14, 2022. https://www.prnewswire.com/news-releases/new-ddi-research-57-percent-of-employees-quit-because-of-their-boss-300971506.html

Step 1: Craft Your Problem Statement

1. https://www.airtimecritical.com/en/helicopter-delivery

2. https://www.airtimecritical.com/en/about

3. Dickson, Andrew. "How we made the Dyson vacuum cleaner." The Guardian. Accessed April 14, 2022. https://www.theguardian.com/culture/2016/may/24/interview-james-dyson-vacuum-cleaner

4. McFadden, Christopher. "James Dyson and His Inventions That Just Work." Interesting Engineering. May 5, 2019. https://interestingengineering.com/james-

dyson-and-his-inventions-that-just-work

5. Probst, Gilbert, PhD. "Better Decision Making: Identify the Real Problem." Wharton Executive Education. Accessed April 14, 2022. https:// executiveeducation.wharton.upenn.edu/thought-leadership/wharton-at-work/ 2015/06/identify-the-real-problem/
6. Llopis, Glenn. "The 4 Most Effective Ways Leaders Solve Problems." Forbes.com. Accessed April 14, 2022. https://www.forbes.com/sites/glennllopis/2013/11/ 04/the-4-most-effective-ways-leaders-solve-problems/

Step 2: Determine The Root Cause Of The Problem

1. Spradlin, Dwayne. "Are You Solving the Right Problem?" Harvard Business Review. Accessed April 14, 2022. https://hbr.org/2012/09/are-you-solving-the-right-problem

Step 4: Problem-Solving

1. Watson, Krista. "3 Ways to Avoid the "Single Story." Progressions.prssa.org. Accessed April 14, 2022. http://progressions.prssa.org/index.php/2016/08/19/3-ways-to-avoid-the-single-story/.
2. Posts by Robin. "Get both sides of the story before you take action on an employee dispute." People Sense Consulting. Accessed April 14, 2022. https://www. peoplesenseconsulting.com/get-both-sides-of-the-story-before-you-take-action-on-an-employee-dispute/
3. Gibbons, Serenity. "You And Your Business Have 7 Seconds To Make A First Impression: Here's How To Succeed." Forbes.com. June 19, 2018. https://www. forbes.com/sites/serenitygibbons/2018/06/19/you-have-7-seconds-to-make-a-first-impression-heres-how-to-succeed/
4. Ibid
5. Lagace, Martha. "Make Your Employees Feel Psychologically Safe." Harvard Business School. November 26, 2018. https://hbswk.hbs.edu/item/make-your-employees-psychologically-safe
6. ibid
7. Berkes, Howard. "Remembering Roger Boisjoly: He Tried to Stop Shuttle Challenger Launch." NPR.com. Accessed April 14, 2022. https://www.npr.org/ sections/thetwo-way/2012/02/06/146490064/remembering-roger-boisjoly-he-tried-to-stop-shuttle-challenger-launch
8. Ibid
9. Asplund, Jim and Blacksmith, Nikki. "The Secret of Higher Performance." Gallup.com. Accessed April 14, 2022. https://news.gallup.com/businessjournal/ 147383/secret-higher-performance.aspx
10. Leadership IQ Website. "Study: The Risks Of Ignoring Employee Feedback." Leadershipiq.com. Accessed April 14, 2022. https://www.leadershipiq.com/ blogs/leadershipiq/study-the-risks-of-ignoring-employee-feedback

11. Ibid
12. Resetera.com Website. "The man who didn't invent flamin' hot cheetos." resetera.com. May 16, 2021. https://www.resetera.com/threads/la-times-the-man-who-didn%E2%80%99t-invent-flamin%E2%80%99-hot-cheetos.426473/
13. Ibid
14. Whalen, Andrew. "The True Story of the Flamin' Hot Cheetos Inventor Richard Montanez." Newsweek.com. August 27, 2019. https://www.newsweek.com/flamin-hot-cheeto-movie-true-story-creator-richard-montanez-1456377
15. Frost, Aja. "Better Brainstorming: The Most Effective Ways To Generate More Ideas." Zapier.com. July 18, 2017. https://zapier.com/blog/brainstorming/

Step 6: The Decision Step

1. Licon, Adriana Gomez and McDermott, Jennifer. "Health officials let COVID-infected staff stay on the job." ABC News. January 10, 2022. https://abcnews.go.com/Health/wireStory/us-hospitals-letting-infected-staff-members-stay-job-82184760
2. Peregrine, Michael. "The Lasting Leadership Lessons From The Challenger Disaster." Forbes.com. January 24, 2021. https://www.forbes.com/sites/michaelperegrine/2021/01/24/the-lasting-leadership-lessons-from-the-challenger-disaster/
3. Ibid
4. Entrepreneur.com Website. "6 Stories of Super Successes Who Overcame Failure." Entrepreneur.com. Accessed April 14, 2022. https://www.entrepreneur.com/article/240492
5. Sherman, Jeremy E. PhD. "Explicit and Implicit Memory: Intuition Training Basics." Psychology Today. Accessed April 14, 2022. https://www.psychologytoday.com/intl/blog/ambigamy/201011/explicit-and-implicit-memory-intuition-training-basics

Step 7: Prepare For Impact

1. Simply Flying Staff. "What Happened To The Airbus A320 That Landed On The Hudson?" Simplyflying.com. August 6, 2020. https://simpleflying.com/miracle-on-the-hudson-aicraft-fate/